Nadzeya Homazava

Micro-capillary ICP-MS technique for corrosion investigations

Nadzeya Homazava

Micro-capillary ICP-MS technique for corrosion investigations

Development of a microflow-capillary set-up online hyphenated to the ICP-MS for the spatial- and time-resolved corrosion investigations

Südwestdeutscher Verlag für Hochschulschriften

Impressum/Imprint (nur für Deutschland/ only for Germany)
Bibliografische Information der Deutschen Nationalbibliothek: Die Deutsche Nationalbibliothek verzeichnet diese Publikation in der Deutschen Nationalbibliografie; detaillierte bibliografische Daten sind im Internet über http://dnb.d-nb.de abrufbar.

Alle in diesem Buch genannten Marken und Produktnamen unterliegen warenzeichen-, marken- oder patentrechtlichem Schutz bzw. sind Warenzeichen oder eingetragene Warenzeichen der jeweiligen Inhaber. Die Wiedergabe von Marken, Produktnamen, Gebrauchsnamen, Handelsnamen, Warenbezeichnungen u.s.w. in diesem Werk berechtigt auch ohne besondere Kennzeichnung nicht zu der Annahme, dass solche Namen im Sinne der Warenzeichen- und Markenschutzgesetzgebung als frei zu betrachten wären und daher von jedermann benutzt werden dürften.

Verlag: Südwestdeutscher Verlag für Hochschulschriften Aktiengesellschaft & Co. KG
Dudweiler Landstr. 99, 66123 Saarbrücken, Deutschland
Telefon +49 681 37 20 271-1, Telefax +49 681 37 20 271-0
Email: info@svh-verlag.de
Zugl.: Bern, Universität, Diss., 2009

Herstellung in Deutschland:
Schaltungsdienst Lange o.H.G., Berlin
Books on Demand GmbH, Norderstedt
Reha GmbH, Saarbrücken
Amazon Distribution GmbH, Leipzig
ISBN: 978-3-8381-1407-1

Imprint (only for USA, GB)
Bibliographic information published by the Deutsche Nationalbibliothek: The Deutsche Nationalbibliothek lists this publication in the Deutsche Nationalbibliografie; detailed bibliographic data are available in the Internet at http://dnb.d-nb.de.

Any brand names and product names mentioned in this book are subject to trademark, brand or patent protection and are trademarks or registered trademarks of their respective holders. The use of brand names, product names, common names, trade names, product descriptions etc. even without a particular marking in this works is in no way to be construed to mean that such names may be regarded as unrestricted in respect of trademark and brand protection legislation and could thus be used by anyone.

Publisher: Südwestdeutscher Verlag für Hochschulschriften Aktiengesellschaft & Co. KG
Dudweiler Landstr. 99, 66123 Saarbrücken, Germany
Phone +49 681 37 20 271-1, Fax +49 681 37 20 271-0
Email: info@svh-verlag.de

Printed in the U.S.A.
Printed in the U.K. by (see last page)
ISBN: 978-3-8381-1407-1

Copyright © 2010 by the author and Südwestdeutscher Verlag für Hochschulschriften Aktiengesellschaft & Co. KG and licensors
All rights reserved. Saarbrücken 2010

For my parents, my brother and my husband.

Table of contents

Abstract 5

Zusammenfassung 7

1. Introduction 9
   1.1. Motivation and goals of the PhD thesis. 9
   1.2. Definition and economical impact of corrosion. 9
   1.3. Types of metal corrosion. 11
   1.4. Introduction into localized corrosion. Passive materials. 13
   1.5. Analytical methods in corrosion science. 16
       1.5.1. Electrochemical techniques. Potentiodynamic polarization method. ... 16
       1.5.2. Surface analytical techniques in corrosion science. 19
       1.5.3. Weight loss measurements and chemical analysis after immersion. ... 23
       1.5.4. Summary: advantages and limitations of analytical techniques used in corrosion science. 26
   1.6. Inductively coupled plasma mass spectrometry. 27
       1.6.1. Standard sample introduction system. 29
       1.6.2. Alternative sample introduction system. 30
       1.6.3. Flow injection sample introduction 31
       1.6.4. ICP ion source. 32
       1.6.5. Interface and ion optics. 32
       1.6.6. Mass analyzer and detector. 34
       1.6.7. Interferences in ICP-MS. 35
   1.7. Scope of the PhD thesis. 36

2. Development of the microflow-capillary system. Offline feasibility corrosion analysis with ICP-MS. 41
   2.1. Overview. 41
   2.2. Experimental. 41
       2.2.1. ICP-MS instrumentation and parameters. 41

1

  2.2.2. Scanning electron microscopy coupled with energy dispersive X-ray analysis (SEM-EDX). 43
  2.2.3. Materials and chemicals. 43
  2.2.4. Sample preparation for ICP-MS analysis. 44

2.3. **Results and discussion.** 44
  2.3.1. Construction of the microflow-capillary set-up. 44
  2.3.2. Analytical optimization of the microflow-capillary set-up. 48
  2.3.3. Application of the offline microflow-capillary set-up for the investigation of micro-corrosion processes in Al alloy 5754. 50

2.4. **Conclusions.** 59

3. Online hyphenation of the microflow-capillary system to ICP-MS using flow injection sample introduction. – An application for *in situ* corrosion characterization of Al alloy 6111. 61

3.1. **Overview.** 61

3.2. **Experimental.** 62
  3.2.1. ICP-MS instrumentation. 62
  3.2.2. Flow injection analysis system. 63
  3.2.3. Data processing. 65
  3.2.4. Materials and chemicals. 65

3.3. **Results and discussion.** 66
  3.3.1. Alternative sample introduction system. 66
  3.3.2. Matrix effects. 70
  3.3.3. Optimization of the flow injection system. 72
  3.3.4. Online time- and element-resolved corrosion investigation of AA 6111. 76

3.4. **Conclusions.** 81

4. Element-specific *in situ* corrosion behaviour of Zr-Cu-Ni-Al-Nb bulk metallic glass in acidic media studied using online microflow-capillary FI-ICP-MS technique. 83

4.1. **Overview.** 83

4.2. **Experimental.** 85
  4.2.1. Microflow-capillary FI-ICP-MS set-up. 85
  4.2.2. X-ray diffraction and X-ray photoelectron spectroscopy. 86
  4.2.3. Materials and chemicals. 87

4.3. **Results and discussion.** 87

4.4. **Conclusions.** 97

5. Online hyphenation of potentiostat to a microflow-capillary FI-ICP-MS for simultaneous *in situ* electrochemical, time and element resolved characterization of local corrosion processes - An application for Zr-bulk metallic glass. 99

   5.1. Overview 99

   5.2. Experimental 100
      5.2.1. Microflow-capillary FI-ICP-MS set-up coupled with the electrochemical control ... 100
      5.2.2. SEM-EDX. 102
      5.2.3. Materials and chemicals. 102

   5.3. Results and discussion 103
      5.3.1. Hyphenation of the potentiostat to the microflow-capillary FI-ICP-MS set-up. Analytical optimization procedure. 103
      5.3.2. Corrosion study on $Zr_{58.5}Cu_{15.6}Ni_{12.8}Al_{10.3}Nb_{2.8}$. Potentiodynamic polarization. 106
      5.3.3. Corrosion study on $Zr_{58.5}Cu_{15.6}Ni_{12.8}Al_{10.3}Nb_{2.8}$. Element- and time resolved online dissolution behaviour monitored with FI-ICP-MS technique under electrochemical control .. 107

   5.4. Conclusions. 115

6. Summary and outlook. 117

7. Abbreviation list 121

8. References. 123

Acknowledgements 133

List of publications 135

Contribution to the conferences and awards 136

Abstract

The thesis was carried out from January 2006 to May 2009 at Empa Swiss Federal Laboratories for Material Testing and Research, in the Laboratory for Analytical Chemistry. Within this thesis, a novel analytical set-up for element specific, spatial- and time-resolved *in situ* analysis of local corrosion processes was developed, optimized and validated. The novel technique is based on the online coupling of a microflow-capillary system to an inductively coupled plasma mass spectrometer (ICP-MS) using online flow injection (FI) sample introduction. Additionally, a three electrode set-up with electrochemical control is adapted to the microflow-capillary FI-ICP-MS set-up for simultaneous chemical and electrochemical characterization of corrosion processes.

Generally, surface and electrochemical methods are mainly used in corrosion science. Surface analytical techniques, predominantly scanning electron microscopy coupled with energy dispersive X-ray analysis (SEM-EDX), provide information only before and after specific corrosion experiment. But these methods are offline and the element-specific quantification of corrosion rates is limited. Furthermore, the surface analysis does not take into account the solution side at the solid-liquid interface during corrosion process.

Electrochemical methods, also extensively used, provide online electrochemical characterization of the corrosion process. However, a major disadvantage of the electrochemical methods is that they provide electrochemical cumulative parameters only, but no information on online element-specific dissolution rates is available.

Thus, a novel technique is needed which allows a detailed element-specific spatial- and time-resolved *in situ* determination of the dissolution processes. The novel microflow-capillary set-up is especially designed for localized *in situ* corrosion experiments and enables a continuous corrosive medium circulation over the investigated material. The construction and optimization of the microflow-capillary are presented in Chapter 2. The coupling of the micro-capillary to ICP-MS using a flow injection system is described in Chapter 3. The coupling allows the sampling of a specific aliquot from the circulating medium and its transient introduction into the plasma mass spectrometer. The adaptation of the electrochemical control to the microflow-capillary FI-ICP-MS set up is presented in Chapter 5. It enables controlled local corrosion provocation and simultaneous electrochemical data acquisition during corrosion processes.

The efficiency of the newly developed technique is proved by several applications using other methods established in corrosion science as a comparison.

On one hand, commercial Al alloys, which are used in automotive and airplane industries, were investigated. On the other hand amorphous zirconium bulk metallic glasses, which belong to prospective new material proposed for biomedical applications, were studied as well. Results of the element-specific corrosion characterization of Al alloys as a function of various experimental conditions are presented in Chapter 2 and Chapter 3. Corrosion susceptibility analysis of Zr-bulk metallic glass with chemical and electrochemical data acquisition is described in Chapter 4 and Chapter 5.

Zusammenfassung

Diese Arbeit wurde in der Zeit von Januar 2006 bis Mai 2009 an der Empa Schweizerischen Materialprüfungs- und Forschungsanstalt in der Abteilung für Analytische Chemie angefertigt. Im Rahmen dieser Dissertation wurde ein neuer analytischer Aufbau zur element-spezifischen, orts- und zeitaufgelösten *in situ* Analyse lokaler Korrosionsprozesse entwickelt, optimiert und validiert. Das neue Analysenverfahren basiert auf einer Mikrofluss-kapillare, die online über ein Fliessinjektionssystem (FI) an ein induktiv gekoppeltes Plasmamassenspektrometer (ICP-MS) gekoppelt wurde. Zusätzlich wurde ein Drei-Elektrodenaufbau mit elektrochemischer Kontrolleinheit in das Mikrofluss-kapillaren FI-ICP-MS System implementiert, um gleichzeitig die Charakterisierung chemischer und elektrochemischer Prozesse während der Korrosion zu untersuchen.

In der Korrosionsforschung werden heute vorwiegend oberflächen- und elektrochemischen Techniken eingesetzt. Oberflächenanalytische Methoden, wobei die Rasterelektronenmikroskopie mit energiedispersiver Röntgenstrahlen-Analyse (REM-EDX) am häufigsten eingesetzt wird, liefern Informationen nur vor und nach einem Korrosionsexperiment. Die Verfahren sind jedoch offline, und die elementspezifische Quantifizierung mittels dieser Techniken sind eingeschränkt. Ausserdem werden Grenzflächenphänomene der flüssig-fest Phase während des Korrosionsprozesses nicht berücksichtigt.

Die ebenfalls stark verbreiteten elektrochemischen Verfahren liefern die Möglichkeit zur online-elektrochemischen Charakterisierung, jedoch besteht ein entscheidender Nachteil dieser Verfahren darin, dass sie nur einen Summenparameter als Mass für die Korrosion liefern. Nützliche Information über die Löslichkeit spezifischer Elemente während der Korrosionsprozesse sind mit diesem Verfahren jedoch nicht zugänglich.

Um auch diese Informationen zu erhalten, bedarf es eines Verfahrens, welches eine elementspezifische, orts- und zeitaufgelöste *in situ* Analyse lokaler Korrosionsprozesse ermöglicht. Die in dieser Arbeit neu entwickelte Mikroflusskapillare wurde speziell für diese Anforderung konstruiert. Damit lokale Korrosionsexperimente durchgeführt werden können, wurde die Mikrofluss-kapillare so konzipiert, dass ein kontinuierlicher Fluss eines gewählten korrosivwirkenden Mediums über eine bestimmte Stelle des zu untersuchenden Material (z.B. Metalllegierungen) fliesst. Die Konstruktion und Optimierung der Mikrofluss-kapillare wird in Kapitel 2 detailliert beschrieben. Kapitel 3 behandelt die online-Kopplung der Mikrofluss-kapillare mit dem ICP-MS über ein FI System. Die Kopplung ermöglicht die Entnahme spezifischer Probenaliquote aus dem zirkulierenden Medium und transiente Einführung in das Plasmamassenspektrometer. Die Implementierung der elektrochemischen Kontrolle in den Mikrofluss-kapillaren FI-ICP-MS Aufbau wird in Kapitel 5 diskutiert. Hierdurch wird eine gezielte Steuerung lokaler Korrosionsprozesse sowie die simultane Aufzeichnung auch elektrochemisch-relevanter Daten während des Korrosionsprozesses ermöglicht.

Die Leistungsfähigkeit es neu entwickelten Analysenverfahrens wurde im Vergleich zu in den Korrosionswissenschaften etablierten Methoden und verschiedenen Anwendungen bewiesen: Untersucht wurde zum einen kommerzielle Aluminiumlegierungen, die in der Automobil- und Luftfahrtindustrie verwendet werden und zum anderen amorphe Zirkonium-basierte metallische Gläser, die als potenzielle neue Materialien beispielsweise für biomedizinische Anwendungen diskutiert werden. Die Ergebnisse der element-spezifische Korrosionsuntersuchungen von verschiedenen Aluminiumlegierungen und bei unterschiedlichen experimentellen Bedingungen finden sich in den Kapiteln 2 und 3. In den Kapiteln 4 und 5 werden die Ergebnisse der Korrosionsexperimente der Zr-Metallgläser und die mit dem Mikrofluss-kapillar FI-ICP-MS Aufbau mit elektrochemischer Kontrolle gewonnenen chemischen und elektrochemischen Daten diskutiert.

1. Introduction.

1.1. Motivation and goals of the PhD thesis.

The main motivation and goal of the PhD thesis was to develop, optimize and validate the novel analytical technique designated for online *in situ* element-specific spatial- and time-resolved investigation of localized corrosion processes in various commercially relevant systems, *e.g.* automotive Al alloys or Zr-based amorphous materials. The development implied the construction of a novel microflow-capillary system for the precise spatial-resolved and local corrosion attack. Moreover, an online hyphenation of the microflow-capillary system to the inductively coupled plasma mass spectrometer using the flow injection sample introduction system should be achieved for transient and online introduction of the corrosion liquid samples into the mass spectrometer instrument. An additional adaptation of the electrochemical control to the developed set-up should furthermore extend the scope of the novel analytical technique with simultaneous chemical and electrochemical data acquisition during the corrosion experiment.

Within the scope of the PhD thesis the novel microflow-capillary FI-ICP-MS technique was validated by comparison to conventional techniques used in corrosion science, *e.g.* scanning electron microscopy coupled with energy dispersive X-ray analysis or X-ray photoelectron spectroscopy. The new technique was applied to the corrosion susceptibility analysis of several industrially used Al alloys (*e.g.* AA 5754, AA 6111) and novel Zr-based bulk metallic glass with a composition of $Zr_{58.5}Cu_{15.6}Ni_{12.8}Al_{10.3}Nb_{2.8}$.

1.2. Definition and economical impact of corrosion.

Corrosion is defined as a process of material degradation due to its reaction with aqueous and/or atmospheric environment. Corrosion is a well known issue in both metal and non-metal materials (concrete, polymers *etc.*), however typically the term "corrosion" refers to metals and metallic systems. Generally, for every corrosion reaction is characteristic the presence of:

a) *anodic site*, where the electrochemical oxidation of the metal is taking place and electrons are produced:

$$M \rightarrow M^{n+} + ne^-$$

b) *cathodic site*, where the reduction of protons or oxygen is taking place and electrons are consumed:

$$2H^+ + 2e^- \rightarrow H_2 \qquad (1.1)$$

$$O_2 + 2H_2O + 4e^- \rightarrow 4OH^- \qquad (1.2)$$

In the anodic reaction the dissolution of the metal occurs, leading to the material degradation. At the cathodic site the reaction 1.1 occurs in acidic aqueous solutions, whereas in solutions with neutral pH the second cathodic reaction of oxygen reduction is the most common (1.2). Since the reactions of anodic oxidation and cathodic reduction occur simultaneously, an electrochemical cell is created in the corrosion process.

To understand the corrosion process of a given material both thermodynamic (corrosion tendency or corrosion driving force) and kinetic (corrosion rate) considerations should be taken into account. The corrosion driving force is defined by the difference in electrochemical potentials between the cathodic and anodic sites of the corrosion. A general estimation of corrosion tendency is possible using Pourbaix equilibrium diagrams, which determine the relation between the potential/pH value and the stability of a given metal [1]. Thus, by means of Pourbaix diagrams it's possible to evaluate, whether the metal will be in the region of immunity, passivity or corrosion. However, the knowledge on corrosion tendency only is not sufficient for thorough characterization of the corrosion process. Hence, the kinetic factor should be also evaluated. Corrosion rate can be determined from the polarization measurements, where current is applied to the metal surface and the potential change is measured.

Corrosion is an important issue in material science and engineering, since it induces enormous damages and yearly costs in billions of US dollars. In the evaluation of the corrosion costs direct and indirect costs are distinguished. Uhlig defined the direct costs as the costs of services and products used for the corrosion prevention, whereas indirect costs are user related and incurred by replacement of corroded materials [2].

In the USA, for example, the yearly direct corrosion costs were estimated to $276 billion [3]. It corresponds to 3.2% of the USA gross domestic product (GDP). Indirect costs to the user (society costs) were conservatively estimated to be equal to the direct costs. Fig. 1.1 illustrates the contribution of the different sectors into the total corrosion costs.

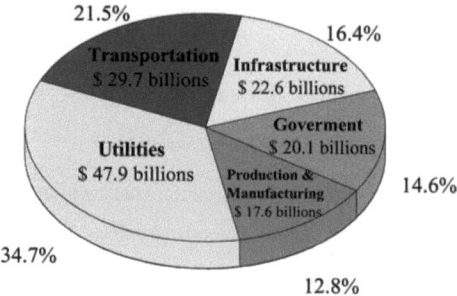

Fig. 1.1. Contribution of different sectors into the total corrosion costs in the USA [3].

In the utility sector, which is responsible for 34.7% of the total corrosion costs, drinking water and sewage systems result in 75% of the costs. About 21.5% of the total costs are transportation related, including the contribution of motor vehicles corrosion and the corrosion in the airplane industry. In Japan, where the studies where limited to evaluation of direct costs only, the corrosion costs were estimated to be on a level of 1.8% of the GDP [4]. In Switzerland, corrosion damage and its consequences result in costs of around 10 billion Swiss franks a year [5].

Corrosion prediction and prevention is necessary not only for economical reasons but also for environmental and safety considerations. Hence, the detailed understanding of corrosion processes and mechanisms is fundamental for an effective prediction and minimization of corrosion damages and the development of resistant materials.

1.3. Types of metal corrosion.

There are several important factors which strongly influence the corrosion behaviour of the material:

a) chemical composition and structure of the material;

b) chemical composition of the corrosive medium;

c) physical and chemical parameters of the environment: temperature, medium flow, oxygen content *etc.*;

d) mechanical forces: friction, tensile strength *etc.*

Due to specific arrangement of anodic and cathodic sites corrosion of material has a specific shape and morphology. According to Fontana [6], corrosion can be categorized into eight different types:

1. *Uniform or General corrosion* is defined as an attack of the material, which occurs uniformly at the entire exposed surface, resulting in a general thinning of the material.

2. *Galvanic corrosion* is corrosion between two dissimilar metals, due to the formation of an electrochemical cell between them. For galvanic corrosion to proceed the metals should have a difference in their electrochemical potential and be in the electrical contact. Moreover, an electrolyte should bridge the metal junction.

3. *Pitting corrosion* is a form of localized corrosion, when small holes (pits) with diameters on a level of tens of micrometers are formed on the surface of a passive metal.

4. *Crevice corrosion* is a second form of localized corrosion, when a stagnant solution with depleted oxygen content or increased acidity occurs in crevices or shielded areas of the material.

5. *Intergranular corrosion* is a selective attack of a material which occurs at the grain boundaries.

6. *Selective corrosion or Selective dealloying* is a preferential dissolution of one or several constituent metals of an alloy. The result of selective corrosion is the formation of porous layer structure.

7. *Stress corrosion cracking* is a cracking of the material due to the joint action of the mechanical stress and corrosive environment. The mechanical stress can be expressed as a direct applied stress or as a residual (internal) stress.

8. *Erosion corrosion* is a gradual degradation of the material due to the combined effect of the corrosion reaction, mechanical wear and abrasion.

1.4. Introduction into localized corrosion. Passive materials.

Localized corrosion (pitting corrosion) is explained more detailed here, since this type of corrosion is mainly studied in this PhD thesis. The main investigated materials were commercial relevant Al alloys and Zr-bulk metallic glasses.

The pitting corrosion susceptibility of so called passive materials is controlled by the formation of a stable surface oxide film.

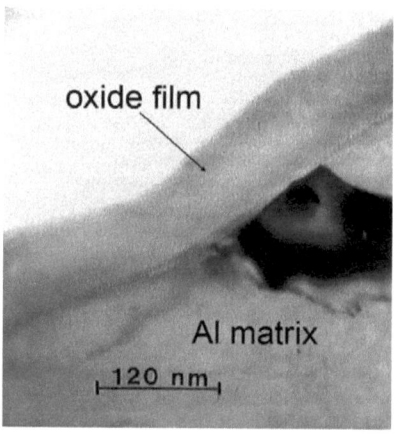

Fig. 1.2. TEM image of the anodic oxide film on pure aluminium in neutral boric acid/sodium borate (the dark part indicates the intermetallic particle) [7].

This film is naturally formed at ambient air. Typically, it has the thickness of 1-10 nm and is highly resistant to corrosive solutions. Both Al alloys and Zr-bulk metallic glasses (Zr-BMG) are characterized as passive materials, where the corrosion attack especially in highly aggressive media like chloride solutions results in the formation of pits. Fig. 1.2 shows a transmission electron microscope (TEM) image of the anodic oxide film on pure aluminium which is formed in neutral boric acid/sodium borate solution [7]. The oxide film is formed on the freshly polished surface immediately, when the sample is exposed to ambient air. Nylund and Olefjord studied the formation of the passive oxide film on Al in dry and humid atmosphere and determined its thickness to be on a level of 1-5 nm [8, 9].

The composition, morphology and properties of the oxide film are strongly dependent on the composition of the material and environment conditions. Influence of the alloying elements on oxide film structure of Al alloys was investigated by Feliu and Bartolomé [10], physical-chemical characteristics of the native oxide film on Al-Mg alloys were studied by Scotto-Sheriff *et al.* [11].

Zr-bulk metallic glasses also belong to the passive materials. They are covered with a thin layer (1-10 nm) of an oxide film at ambient air. X-ray photoelectron spectroscopy (XPS) analysis of Zr-BMG oxide films revealed its complex composition with predominance of Zr- and Al-oxides in the film [12, 13]. However, also secondary elements can be present in the oxide composition.

According to Szklarska-Smialowska [14], four stages of pitting corrosion can be distinguished:

1) process occurring on the passive film, at the boundary of the passive film and corrosive solution;
2) processes occurring within the passive film;
3) formation of metastable pits, which appear and grow for a short time and then repassivate;
4) stable pit growth above the critical pitting potential.

Pitting corrosion usually initiates at weakest locations, normally surface defects, crevices, intermetallic particles (IMPs) or segregations. The localization of aggressive corrosive environments which proceeds at these locations causes the breakdown of the corrosion resistant surface film and leads to the pits formation.

Pitting corrosion of Al alloys. In the case of Al alloys, for example, pitting corrosion is caused mainly by alloy microstructure heterogeneity, *i.e.* by the presence of IMPs. Different alloying elements like Fe, Cu, Mg, Mn, and Si are added to modify the physical properties and strengthen the alloy. Some of these elements are then present in small dispersoids and in large intermetallic particles (1-20 µm) formed because of the element segregation during the cooling of the alloy. These large intermetallics are the main reason for an acceleration of corrosion processes. Potential difference between the matrix and intermetallics present in the alloy leads to the galvanic coupling. Moreover, intermetallic particles exhibit different surface film characteristics as compared to the alloy matrix. Other alloying elements like Mg can also be present in the bulk of Al-phase, due to the formation of solid solution with Al matrix.

Fig. 1.3 shows anodic and cathodic reactions, which are common for pitting corrosion of Al alloys. Al(Fe,Mn) intermetallics, which belong to the typical cathodic IMPs and have the electrochemical potential higher than the bulk alloy, provoke aluminium matrix dissolution around them. Mg_2Si particles, also very common for Al alloys, serve as local anodes and undergo the active dissolution process due to the lower electrochemical potential as compared to the Al matrix.

Introduction

The influence of the intermetallic particles, which are typically present in different commercial Al alloys, on the corrosion propagation was studied by various authors. Birbilis and Buchheit presented a comprehensive survey on corrosion potentials, pitting potentials, and electrochemical characteristics for IMPs commonly present in commercial Al alloys [15].

It was proved that the electrochemical behaviour of the intermetallics is strongly dependent upon their chemical composition. Thus, particles, which contain Cu, Fe or Ti, *e.g.* Al_3Fe, Al_7Cu_2Fe, Al_2Cu and Al_3Ti exhibit more noble behaviour than pure Al or Al alloy matrix.

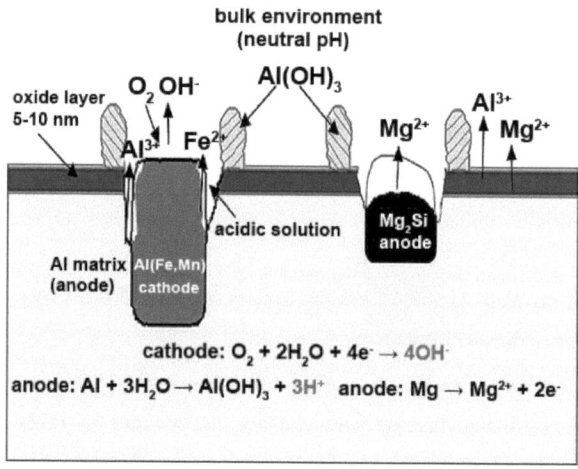

Fig. 1.3. Scheme of possible anodic and cathodic reactions during pitting corrosion of a typical Al alloy with Mg, Fe, Si, Mn secondary alloying elements.

Contrary, intermetallics, which have Mg or Zn in their composition, *e.g.* $MgZn_2$, Mg_2Si are typically less noble than pure Al or Al alloy matrix and corrode freely above their corrosion potential. Moreover, the corrosion behaviour of the IMPs is strongly influenced not only by their chemical composition but also by the pH value of the corrosive solution [16].

Pitting corrosion of Zr-bulk metallic glasses. An enhanced corrosion resistance of Zr-bulk metallic glasses is attributed to the strong passivation ability of Zr. However, Zr-BMGs as well as Al alloys are highly prone to pitting corrosion in chloride-containing solutions. The high corrosion susceptibility in this case is attributed to the fact that the cast structure of the bulk metallic glasses is not free from the defects. During the process of slow cooling in copper mold casting, trace impurities, which may be present in the melt, can lead to the formation of crystalline phases. Thus, the interface between the crystalline inclusion and the glass matrix can serve as a preferential site of Cl^- ions adsorption, which provokes the oxide film breakdown and pitting initiation. Afterwards, pit growth propagates into the highly reactive BMG matrix, while the small crystalline inclusion remains mainly unattached and can deattach from the surface [17].

Summarizing the key points presented in this paragraph, it is worth to highlight that the material susceptibility to pitting corrosion depends on a number of factors:

a) chemical composition and microstructure of the material;

b) the characteristics of the surface oxide film and the presence of intermetallic inclusions;

c) the chemical composition of the corrosive solution, especially the concentration of aggressive ions;

d) temperature.

1.5. Analytical methods in corrosion science.

1.5.1. Electrochemical techniques. Potentiodynamic polarization method.

As it was explained above, the mechanism of corrosion at the metal/environment interface is an electrochemically driven process. That is why electrochemical techniques are most extensively used in corrosion research. The theoretical principles of the electrochemical techniques are well established. Electrochemical methods can provide comprehensive electrochemical information on corrosion processes and can be used both in the laboratory and in the field. The measurements are fast and are sensitive to low corrosion rates. The measurement of the current, which can be performed down to the femtoampere level with the most recent electrochemical systems, gives by far the highest detection limit in terms of corrosion initiation investigation. However, electrochemical techniques give only cumulative parameters which characterize the corrosion process:

– pitting potential, E_{pit};

– open circuit potential, E_{ocp};

– current density values, i.

Introduction

Electrochemical measurement are usually conducted in three-compartment *electrochemical cell*, using the investigated sample in contact with the corrosive solution as a *working electrode* (WE), while the *reference electrode* (RE) and the *counter electrode* (CE) are immersed into the same corrosive solution. A prerequisite is the conductivity of the material.

Potential measurement. The potential of the working electrode (metal sample) is measured against the reference electrode. To attribute the potential measurements to the changes, which occur at the surface of the metal sample during its reaction with corrosive environment, measurements against a stable reference electrode are required. To be used in the electrochemical cell the RE should meet the following requirements:

a)   a reproducible potential;

b)   a stable potential;

c)   convenient and durable construction.

A silver-silver chloride RE (Ag/AgCl/1M KCl RE, E_{SHE} = + 0.235 V) and saturated calomel RE (Hg/Hg_2Cl_2/saturated KCl RE, E_{SHE} = + 0.280 V, SCE) are among the most typical RE used in the electrochemical measurements in corrosion science [18].

Current measurement. Current measurements are performed in order to estimate the current which flows between two components of the electrochemical cell. The current is measured between the WE and CE.

Polarization measurements include the measurement of the relation between the electrochemical potential and the corrosion current. Among the different electrochemical techniques, polarization methods (*e.g.*, potentiodynamic, potentiostatic or galvanostatic) are most often used. In potentiostatic measurements the potential of an electrode is controlled and the response of current is monitored. If the potential is being changed at a constant rate and the response of the current is continuously monitored then the method is called potentiodynamic.

Thus, in the potentiodynamic polarization method, the sample is being polarized, *i.e.* the potential is applied to the sample starting from the open circuit potential (E_{ocp}) or from cathodic prepolarization. The potential is scanned in the noble direction together with the continuous monitoring of the current density values. At the pitting potential, E_{pit}, the anodic current increases sharply, thus providing a simple measurement of E_{pit}. Fig. 1.4 presents a typical polarization curve of the passive material (indicating E_{ocp}, E_{pit} and repassivation potential, E_{rep}).

The spectrum of the investigations in the field of classical electrochemical techniques is so broad, that no full review can be given within this introduction. However, recently proposed *local probe electrochemical techniques* for more precise and detailed investigation of local corrosion processes should be mentioned.

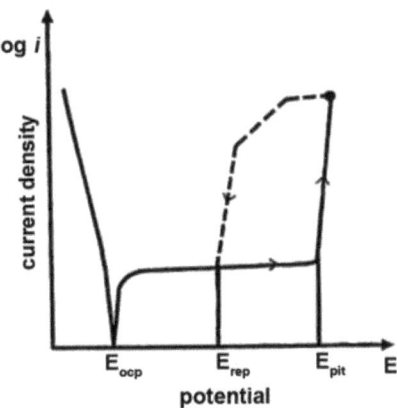

Fig. 1.4. Schematic polarization curve.

Micro-electrochemical set-up based on a static microcapillary electrochemical measurement was developed by T. Suter (Empa) and H. Böhni [19-21]. The static microcapillary, containing a RE and a CE is filled with the corrosive solution and installed instead one of the objectives into an optical microscope. Using the positioning manipulator of the optical microscope the capillary can be adjusted at the specific spot of the sample. The tip of the capillary can usually have a diameter of about 1-100 µm, and is additionally sealed with silicon rubber gel to prevent the leaking of the solution from the static capillary.

This set-up was applied for the investigation of local corrosion processes in various systems, *e.g.* studies on pit initiation of high purity and ultra high purity aluminium [22], stainless steel in NaCl solutions [23] or Al alloy 2024-T3 [24]. The set-up has a lateral resolution in the lower micrometer range, but most recent investigations also reached the sub-micrometer range down to a minimum diameter of 300 nm [25]. Similar or slightly modified static micro-capillary electrochemistry techniques were also adapted by other groups later on [26-28].

Several combined microprobe techniques, which include a combination of the microelectrochemical cell with other physical or chemical technique (*e.g.* pH-sensor, SEM *etc.*), have been developed to characterize the processes at the metal-solution interface associated with localized corrosion. The combination of the micro-electrochemical capillary set-up and pH microsensor was presented in [29]. It was employed to investigate simultaneously the local pH changes and current transients on stainless steel AISI 304 SS in 0.1 M NaCl solution. Paik and Alkire developed a combination of scanning electrochemical microscopy and the microelectrochemical cell in order to demonstrate the role of adsorbed sulphur species near sulphide inclusions as a driving force of nickel pitting [30].

From these examples it is evident that combination of local techniques provides more detailed and thorough characterization of corrosion processes and gives a deeper understanding of corrosion mechanisms. As it was highlighted by Oltra *et al.* [31], the future trend will be to develop specific multifunctional probes allowing simultaneous measurement of electrochemical, chemical and topographical changes during corrosion.

1.5.2. Surface analytical techniques in corrosion science.

Surface analytical techniques like Scanning Electron Microscopy coupled with Energy Dispersive X-ray analysis (SEM-EDX), X-ray photoelectron spectroscopy or Auger electron spectroscopy (AES) are often used methods in corrosion research. Surface techniques are mainly used to study variations and changes in material and passive oxide film compositions, which occur after the corrosion process. The influence of corrosion is usually determined by a comparison of samples before and after corrosion experiment. Different corrosion phenomena have been described using various surface analytical techniques, focussing on optical appearance of resulting surface topography, pitting initiation, pit propagation and growth.

These methods enable characterization of materials surface comprising different spatial resolution and detection power. Characteristic properties of the most common surface analytical techniques used in corrosion research in terms of spatial and depth resolution, information depth, detection limits, multi-element detection capabilities, information, whether the method is destructive or non-destructive (due to sputtering or ablation of the sample material) are summarized in Table 1.

Table 1. Properties of surface sensitive element analytical techniques (approx. ranges) [32-35].

Technique	Detection limit	Multi-element detection	Chemical bonding information	Lateral resolution	Depth resolution		Destructive?
					Surface depth	Depth profiling	
SEM-EDX	0.1-1% 1-10 mg/g	yes	no	0.3 µm	0.5-3 µm	no	no
TEM-EDX	0.1-1% 1-10 mg/g	yes	no	<0.2 nm	0.5-3 µm	no	no
XPS	0.05% 0.5 mg/g	yes	yes extensive	150 µm	2 nm	0.5 µm	no
AES	0.1-1%	yes	yes considerable	50 nm	2 nm	2 µm	no
SIMS	0.0001% <1 µg/g	yes	yes poor	1 µm	1 nm	10 µm	(no)
AFM	-	yes	no	1.5-5 nm	0.01 nm	no	no
LA-ICP-MS	<1 µg/g	yes	no	10-100 µm	100-1000 nm	1-5 µm	yes

Characterization of sample surfaces provides information on depletion of certain elements, which might be dissolved during a corrosion attack. But a possible enhancement/depletion of specific elements can only be detected by a comparison of results achieved before and after the corrosion experiment. Thus, most surface analytical techniques used in corrosion research are offline and do not take into account the solution side of the solid-liquid interface that is always present during the corrosion process. Therefore, a time depending change in a chemical composition or an element depending dissolution progress cannot be directly investigated. The time-resolved investigation can only be achieved combining the corrosion experiments performed on different samples, which is a highly time-consuming procedure.

Although the elemental sensitivity of the method is limited, SEM-EDX is probably the most often used technique to study corroded samples. The technique is primary used for providing images of the microstructural changes, which occur during corrosion.

More surface sensitive methods like XPS or AES give much more information on oxidation, passivation and compositional changes of the oxide film related to corrosion processes. Using XPS method both the thin oxide film layer and the metal surface underneath may be examined. XPS signals of the metal are generally sufficiently separated from those of the oxide film due to the chemical shifts [36]. Moreover, beside the chemical analysis of the oxide film, XPS allows the studies on chemical bonding and oxidation states. However, analysis by XPS is limited in spatial resolution (~ 150 µm). Consequently, a surface technique with sub-micron spatial resolution is as necessary as chemical characterization. Thus, AES which uses a sub-micron electron beam as a probe, is considered to have the equal importance in corrosion studies [33].

Analysis of concentration profiles as a function of depth achieved with AES can reveal gradients which can lead to an explanation of film growth mechanisms. Predominantly, depth profiling option in AES is used to determine:

a) the thickness of the oxide;

b) the distribution of the metallic cations derived from the alloy;

c) the position and enrichment of any aggressive anions (*e.g.*, chloride, sulphide) relative to the oxygen profile [36].

The main advantage of AES beside its lateral resolution is also a fast data acquisition. However, both XPS and AES clearly focus on the characterization of the solid part of the solid-liquid interface involved in the corrosion processes occurring on the passive oxide film.

Laser ablation inductively coupled plasma mass spectrometry (LA-ICP-MS) is also a useful method for depth profile analysis, investigation of elements diffusion from the alloy into a corrosive-resistant coating [37] or quantitative elements mapping of certain metallic alloys [38-40], which are of great importance in corrosion science.

Moreover, Secondary Ion Mass Spectrometry (SIMS) can also provide useful information in corrosion studies. The method is based on the mass spectrometric detection of ions emitted from the surface during its bombardment with a particle beam. Mass analysis of the atomic and molecular particles sputtered from the surface enables the determination of the surface composition. Therefore, element-resolved in-depth film profiles can be obtained from SIMS measurements [32]. Moreover, when the electrochemical experiments are performed in ^{18}O-containing solutions, SIMS analysis is employed to evaluate the air stability of the formed oxide film. If the film is unstable, it will pick up ^{16}O from the air, revealing a decreased ^{18}O content compared to the solution as detected by SIMS [34].

Various surface analytical techniques were applied for the corrosion studies in Al alloys and Zr-BMGs. For example, the combination of electrochemical measurements and SEM-EDX surface characterization before and after corrosion was applied for the corrosion characterization of Al alloy (AA) 7075 [41], where the corrosion initiation was attributed to Cu- and Fe-rich intermetallics. Additionally, the sample was characterized by Scanning Kelvin Probe Force Microscopy (SKPFM) to reveal the potential difference between the particles of different composition. Guillaumin and Mankowski [42] investigated localized corrosion behaviour of AA 6065 T6 aluminium alloy using the combination of polarisation measurements, SEM and TEM observation and Phase Shifting Interferometric Microscopy (PSIM, investigation of intermetallic reactivity through construction of 2D and 3D profiles); coarse Al-Si-Mg intermetallics were found to be the nucleation sites for pits. The role of intermetallic phases in localized corrosion of AA 5083 Al alloy was studied with SEM-EDX and Atomic Force Microscopy (AFM) methods [43]. SEM-EDX was also employed for microconstituent-induced pitting corrosion investigation in Al alloy 2024-T3 [44].

Electrochemical measurements combined with microscopic observations are also well established techniques and typically used for corrosion susceptibility studies of Zr-bulk metallic glasses [45-48]. Moreover, depth profiles of anodically passivated sample surfaces were investigated using AES analysis [46, 49]. Hiromoto *et al.* [50, 51] employed XPS method to characterize the chemical composition of the surface oxide film of non-polarized and polarized $Zr_{65}Al_{7.5}Ni_{10}Cu_{17.5}$ sample;

Qiu *et al.* [52] described the effect of Nb addition on oxide film structure of ZrAlCuNi bulk metallic glass after polarization in a passive region using XPS.

Thus, common surface analytical techniques provide valuable information in corrosion research. However, in most cases the sample is characterized *ex situ*, *i.e.* before and after corrosion experiment.

1.5.3. Weight loss measurements and chemical analysis after immersion.

Quantification of dissolution rates is possible using weight loss measurements [53, 54], which are usually performed as bulk immersion tests. The bulk sample is immersed in the corrosive solution for a certain time and the difference in the sample mass before and after the immersion is determined afterwards. However, weight loss measurements provide neither element-specific information on the corrosion process, nor do they allow distinguishing between impacts of specific alloying elements into a total weight loss of the sample.

Thus, element-depending information or quantification of element-resolved dissolution rates from the material into the corrosive medium at metal-liquid interface can only be obtained by chemical analysis.

At the end of the 1980s - beginning of the 1990s methods like atomic absorption spectrometry (AAS) and ion chromatography (IC) were proposed for the chemical analysis of corrosion dissolution processes. However, the sensitivity of these methods was not sufficient to thoroughly characterize the element-resolved dissolution rates of secondary alloying elements present in the alloy in sub-percent quantities.

That is why in the past ten years plasma spectrochemistry methods like inductively coupled plasma optical emission spectrometry (ICP-OES) and *inductively coupled plasma mass spectrometry (ICP-MS)* [55, 56] have gained an increasing interest in corrosion related investigations. Characteristics like fast multi-element detection capability, high sensitivity and low detection limits provide excellent possibilities for simultaneous multi-element monitoring of dissolution processes during corrosion (a detailed description of the ICP-MS method is provided in the Chapter 1.5.). However, there are few publications on the application of ICP-MS in the corrosion research up to now. Usually, an investigated sample is immersed in the corrosive medium for a specified time with ICP-MS analysis of the medium afterwards. In this case, ICP-MS analysis is performed as an offline bulk analysis, characterizing the total metal release from the material with no detailed information

Introduction

on spatial and time-resolved nature of corrosion mechanisms. Applications of chemical analysis techniques in corrosion studies are presented in Table 2.

A clear transition from single-element and sequential chemical analysis methods to simultaneous multi-element detection of elements released from the material with a high detection power and low detection limits is observed over the past two decades (Table 2). However only few publications describe online element-specific characterization of corrosion dissolution processes, like the development of a flow cell coupled with an ICP-OES/ICP-MS for *in situ* chemical analysis. However in this case the exposed metal surface is large and the corrosion mechanisms are investigated on a macro-scale level only.

Table 2. Application of chemical analysis techniques in corrosion studies.

Technique	Immersion test	Material	Multi-element detection capability	Reference
Fluorometric method	Bulk immersion offline	AA 2024-T3	No single-element sensitivity (Al only)	[57, 58]
AAS **Atomic Absorption Spectrometry**	Bulk immersion offline	Orthodontic brackets (stainless steel)	No Sequential analysis Ni, Cr, Fe, Mn	[59]
		Bronzes	No Sequential analysis Cu, Sn, Zn, Pb	[60]
		AA 7075 T6	No Al	[61]
		350 stainless steel (SS)	No Sequential analysis Ni, Cr, Fe	[62]
IC **Ion Chromatography**	Bulk immersion offline	304 SS, 316 SS	Yes Cr, Ni, Fe Mn	[63]

ICP-OES Inductively Coupled Plasma Optical Emission Spectrometry	Bulk immersion Offline	Al oxide on high pure Al	Yes Al	[64]
		Metallic biomaterial	Yes Ca, Ti, Fe, Cr, Ni, Co, etc.	[65]
		Dental ceramics	Yes Na, K, Mg, Ca, Ba, Ti, etc	[66]
	Bulk immersion flow cell (online)	304 SS, Fe-Cr alloys	Yes Fe Cr, Ni, Mn, Mo, Cu	[67, 68]
ICP-MS Inductively Coupled Plasma Mass Spectrometry	Bulk immersion Offline	304 SS, 254 SMO SS	Yes Ni, Cr, Fe, Mo	[69, 70]
		Dental alloys Pd-Cu-Ga alloy	Yes Pd, Ga, Cu, Sn, Ag, In, Ru	[71]
		Ni-Cr, Co-Cr alloys	Ni, Cr, Fe	[72]
		Zr-BMG	Yes Ni Cu, Zr, Nb, Fe, Cu	[73]
		WC-Co	Yes W, Co	[74]
	Bulk immersion flow cell (online)	WC-Co	Yes W, Co	[75]

Thus, up to now, localized online element- and spatial-resolved chemical analysis of corrosion processes is not available. Hence, a development of a novel analytical technique, which combines simultaneous online multi-element detection capability with a local spatially resolved corrosion attack, is crucial for a thorough understanding of corrosion mechanisms. An additional adaptation of an electrochemical control would allow online chemical and electrochemical characterization of corrosion at the same time.

Introduction

The goal of the planned analytical technique for corrosion investigations is to combine the excellent spatial capabilities of a microflow-capillary set-up with the high sensitivity of ICP-MS including online flow injection (FI) sample introduction system. The detailed description of the thesis scope and idea of the novel *microflow-capillary FI-ICP-MS technique with the electrochemical control* are given in the Chapter 1.6.

1.5.4. Summary: advantages and limitations of analytical techniques used in corrosion science.

Table 3 presents an overview of advantages and limitation of different analytical techniques commonly used in corrosion research.

Table 3. Advantages and drawbacks of common analytical methods applied in corrosion science.

Analytical technique	Online	Electro-chemical information	Element-specific chemical information	Local	Material independent
Electrochemical analysis	yes	yes	no	yes	no conductivity is mandatory
Surface techniques	no	no	yes quantification is limited	yes	yes
Bulk immersion tests	no	no	yes	no	yes
Microflow-capillary FI-ICP-MS + electrochemical control	*yes* via FI sample introduction	*yes* via Electro-chemical control	*yes* via ICP-MS	*yes* via Microflow-capillary	*yes*

1.6. Inductively coupled plasma mass spectrometry.

Inductively coupled plasma mass spectrometry, first introduced in the beginning of 1980s by two different working groups, *i.e.* by Houk and co-workers [76]; and by Date and Gray [77]. ICP-MS is nowadays a widely used ultra-trace analysis technique which provides fast simultaneous multi-element detection capability over a wide linear dynamic range and high detection power. It enables the element analysis down to sub-ng L^{-1} range [55].

Fig. 1.5 shows the linear dynamic range of ICP-MS in comparison to other common analytical techniques. As it can be seen, in ICP-MS trace, minor and major elements can be simultaneously quantified, due to the fact that the linear range covers nine orders of magnitude.

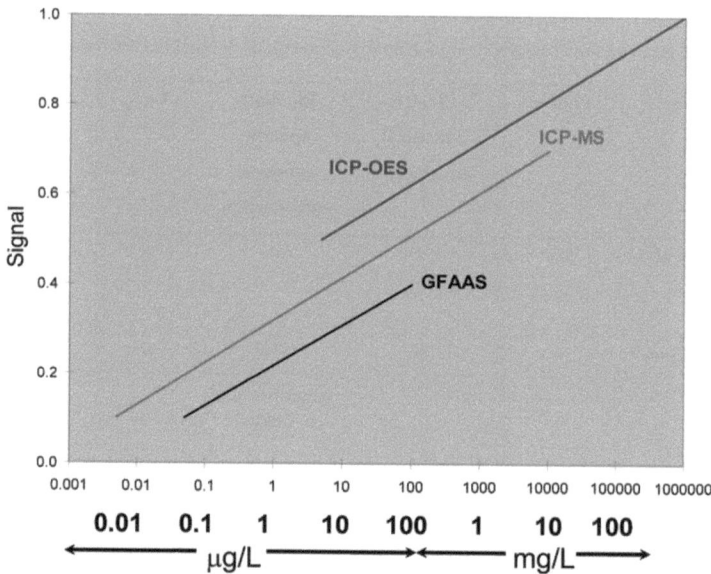

Fig. 1.5. Dynamic linear range of ICP-MS in comparison to other analytical techniques.

The detection limits typical for a ELAN 6000 quadrupole ICP-MS instrument are presented in Fig. 1.6 and lie in the range of 1-10 ng L^{-1} for most elements analyzed.

Introduction

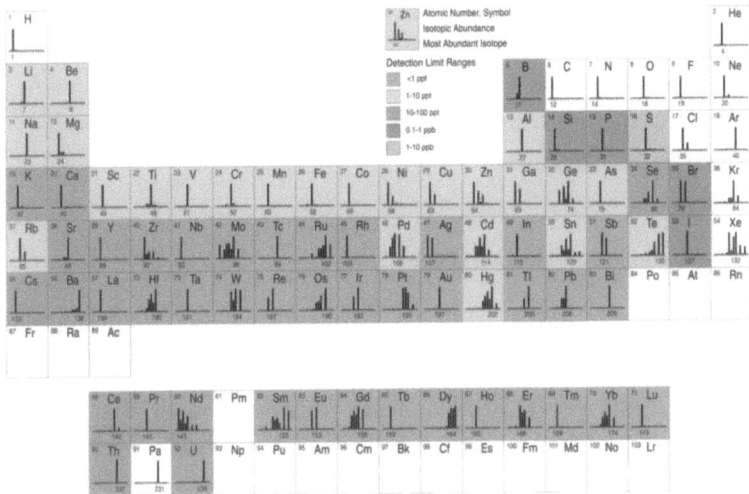

Fig. 1.6. Detection capabilities of ELAN 6000 quadrupole ICP-MS (Courtesy of PerkinElmer).

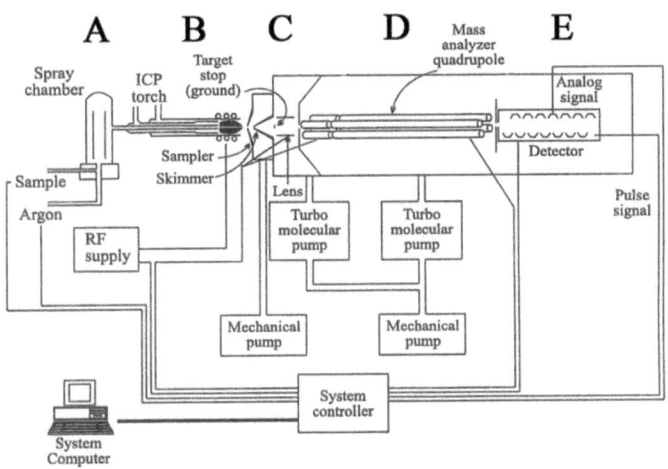

Fig. 1.7. Schematic diagram of a quadrupole ICP-MS ELAN 6000: A. sample introduction system; B. ICP ion source; C. interface; D. mass analyzer; E. detector [55].

An ICP-MS instrument consists of five integral parts (A. sample introduction system; B. ICP ion source; C. interface; D. mass analyzer; E. detector), as demonstrated in Fig. 1.7. In the present PhD thesis the development of the novel microflow-capillary analytical technique for corrosion investigations and its coupling to the ICP-MS spectrometer were performed for the quadrupole ICP-MS ELAN 6000 (Perkin Elmer/Sciex).

1.6.1. Standard sample introduction system.

The standard sample introduction system for liquid sample analysis in ICP-MS includes the generation of the aerosol from the liquid by a nebulizer, separation of fine droplets of the aerosol from coarsest droplets by a spray chamber and, finally, introduction of the fine aerosol into the plasma. Efficiency and accuracy of the sample introduction system has a significant influence on the quality of the analytical results, since the transformation of the liquid sample into the aerosol has to be stoichiometrical.

A typical sample introduction system consists of a pneumatic nebulizer (where the liquid sample is transformed into the aerosol using the high velocity argon gas stream) and a spray chamber. The main process taking place in the spray chamber is the separation of coarse droplets from the primary fine aerosol, resulting in the tertiary aerosol, which is finer and less polydisperse.

Conventional sample introduction systems are known to have several limitations, when used in ICP-MS [78]:

a) the sample transport efficiency is very low, *i.e.* only about 2-5% of the sample reaches the plasma, the rest of the aerosol droplets are too coarse and they are drained to the waste);

b) long wash-out times and high memory effects;

c) the relatively high liquid sample consumption of about 1 ml min^{-1} is a limitation for the analysis of low volume liquid samples (< 1 ml).

Thus, in case of the microflow-capillary system developed in the PhD thesis, an alternative sample introduction system is needed for analysis of low volume corrosion samples (20-100 µl) with high salt content [79, 80].

1.6.2. Alternative sample introduction system.

For the corrosion samples analysis in the microflow-capillary FI-ICP-MS technique an alternative low sample volume introduction system was installed into the ICP-MS instrument. It consists of a pneumatic concentric micronebulizer Micromist [81] and a low inner volume spray chamber Cinnabar [82].

In comparison to the conventional pneumatic nebulizer Micromist microconcentric nebulizer (MMN) has reduced capillary dimensions (inner diameter and wall thickness), which leads to the more efficient interaction between the liquid sample and Ar gas stream and consequently to finer primary aerosols. Todoli *et al.* demonstrated that Micromist nebulizer shows an efficient and accurate performance at sample uptake rates < 100 μl min^{-1} [83, 84]. However, at such low flow rates, the wash-out times found for conventional spray chambers are significantly increased. Low inner volume minicyclonic spray chamber (20 cm^3) Cinnabar demonstrated significantly shorter wash-out times in comparison with a conventional cyclonic spray chamber (40 cm^3) [82, 85]. Fig. 1.8 shows a scheme of the alternative sample introduction system.

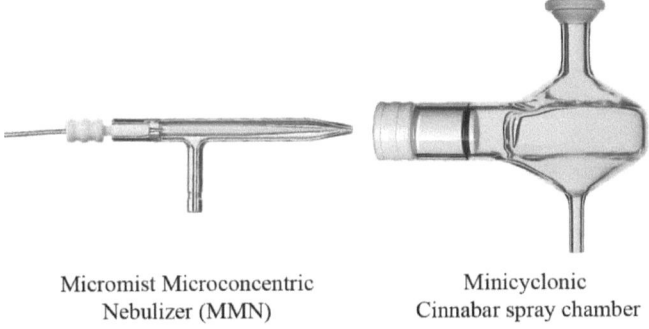

Micromist Microconcentric Nebulizer (MMN)   Minicyclonic Cinnabar spray chamber

Fig. 1.8. Micromist microconcentric nebulizer in a conjunction with a Cinnabar spray chamber [81].

These advantages of the alternative sample introduction system come along with the requirements for the analysis of low volume corrosion samples in the microflow-capillary FI-ICP-MS technique. However, the performance characteristic of Micromist nebulizer in conjunction with a Cinnabar spray chamber had to be optimized for the corrosion samples analysis.

Other alternative sample introduction system suitable for the analysis of liquid microsamples in ICP-OES and ICP-MS have been described in a comprehensive review of J. L. Todoli and J. M. Mermet [86].

1.6.3. Flow injection sample introduction.

Flow injection analysis was introduced by Růžička and Hansen in 1975 [87]. The technique is based on the injection of a small sample aliquot into an unsegmented carrier stream. Typically, a flow injection sample introduction system contains a switching valve with a sample loop and a peristaltic pump, both operated by a computer. A loop in the valve is automatically filled with a liquid sample. At a specified time moment the valve is switched and the content of the sample loop is introduced into the carrier stream which leads to the ICP-MS instrument. Fig. 1.9 shows an overview of a typical flow injection sample introduction system.

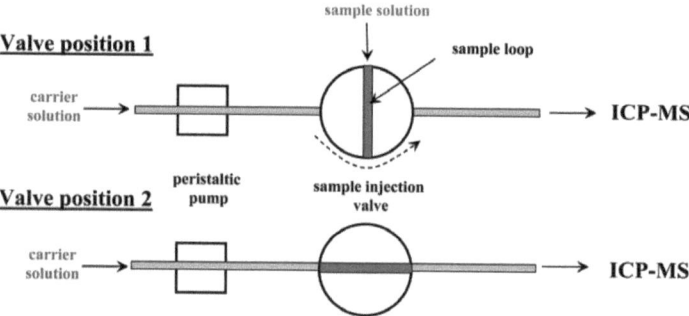

Fig. 1.9. Overview of a typical flow injection sample introduction system.

Combined with the ICP-MS detection flow injection sample introduction system offers important advantages over traditional continuous sample introduction system. The sample liquid volume introduced into the carrier stream is significantly minimized due to use of the sample loop (20-100 µl), thus making analysis of low volume samples possible and reducing the matrix load on the mass spectrometer instrument, when samples with a high total dissolved salt content are analyzed [88-90].

1.6.4. ICP ion source.

The tertiary aerosol leaving the spray chamber is introduced into the plasma through the central sample injector of the ICP torch. Most ICP-MS instruments use Scott-Fassel-type ICP torch first introduced in 1974 for ICP-OES [91]. The torch consists of three concentric tubes (18 mm, outer tube; 13 mm, middle tube; and 1.5 mm central sample injector). The outer gas flow (coolant gas flow) protects the tube walls and serves as the main plasma support gas with a flow of usually 10-15 L min^{-1}. The auxiliary gas is introduced between the middle and the central tubes at the flow of 0-1 L min^{-1} and is mainly used to prevent the melting of the central aerosol injector tube and the quartz torch. The aerosol flows into the ICP torch from the spray chamber with a velocity of 0.5-1.5 L min^{-1}. At the outer top the torch is encircled by a load coil (made from copper) connected to the radiofrequency generator (RF) (27.12 MHz or 40.68 MHz), which is used for heating the plasma. When RF power is applied to the coil, an oscillating current is produced at the rate which corresponds to the frequency of the generator. The current oscillation produces a strong electromagnetic field at the top of the torch. Free electrons produced through a discharge in a cold torch by a Tesla spark are accelerated by the RF magnetic field leading to the numerous collisions with Ar atoms and ionization of Ar gas. [78, 92]. When the sample aerosol is introduced into highly energetic Ar plasma (6000-1000 K) it is being transformed into the ions through consequent desolvation, vaporization, atomization and ionization steps. Since Ar has a relatively high first ionization potential (15.8 eV), the ionization of most elements to more than 90% is possible in the Ar plasma. However, elements which have the first ionization potential higher than Ar (F, Ne and He) and elements which have the ionization potential close to Ar (*e.g.* Br, Cl, N, O) are not ionizable or ionizable only to a certain percentage in Ar plasma.

1.6.5. Interface and ion optics.

The role of the interface is to extract ions formed in the ICP torch and to transfer them into the mass separation side of the ICP-MS instrument. The ion extraction includes transporting of analyte ions from high temperature (~ 7500 K) and ambient pressure (~ 1 bar or 100 kPa) into a high vacuum (~ $10^{-5} - 10^{-9}$ bar or $1 \cdot 10^{-4}$ Pa) mass separation part operating at room temperature (~ 300 K). For this purpose all commercial ICP-MS instruments employ a similar sampling interface, the main part of it being the sampler and the skimmer cones (Fig. 1.10).

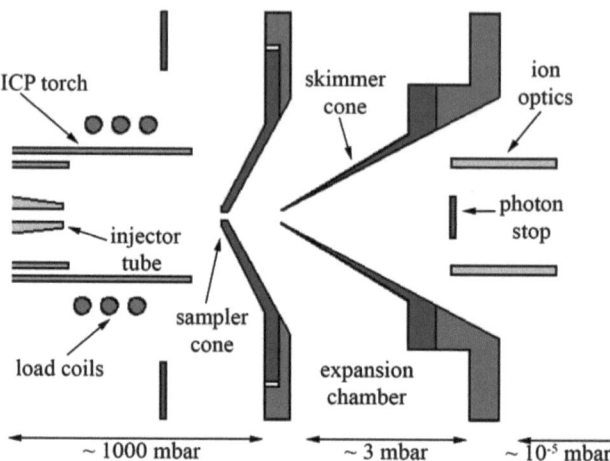

Fig. 1.10. A cross section of a typical ICP-MS sampling interface.

The ICP flame is centred on the first sampling aperture with a typical opening diameter of 0.5-1 mm. The cones are usually manufactured from nickel or platinum. Since the cones suffer from the sample matrix condensation during the prolonged use, they have to be easily exchanged for cleaning. That is why the cones are replaceable and usually retained by screws. The plate which holds the sampler cone is water cooled to prevent the melting of the cone.

Behind the front aperture the second cone (named skimmer cone) is placed. The space between the sampler and skimmer cones is called an expansion chamber, where the reduced pressure of ~ 3 mbar is produced using a rotary pump. Due to the creation of this reduced pressure region the plasma is drawn into the expansion chamber. The skimmer cone is used to extract the ions from the expansion chamber into the high vacuum region. Behind the skimmer cone the ion lens system, consisting of photon stop and ion lenses, is placed. The photon stop is used to prevent the photons entering the mass analyzer and reaching the detector.

The main purpose of the ion lenses is to focus the ion beam and transport it after the charge separation to the mass analyzer with a maximum transmission.

1.6.6. Mass analyzer and detector.

Various mass analyzers can be implemented in the ICP-MS instrument. The most commonly used mass analyzer is the quadrupole mass filter (installed in ~90% of all commercially used instruments) [93, 94]. ELAN 6000 belongs also to the quadrupole ICP-MS instrument type.

A typical quadrupole mass filter consists of four straight metal rods (made from stainless steel or molybdenum) arranged in parallel pairs along the axis and equidistant from the axis. Opposite pairs are connected together. To the one of the pairs the potential of +(U+Vcos(wt)) is applied, whereas to the other pair the potential applied is -(U+Vcos(wt)). The direct current (DC) voltage has the amplitude U and the RF voltage has the amplitude V. The DC voltage is positive for one pair and negative for the other. The trajectory of the ion flying through the quadrupole mass filter depends on the applied voltages. For a given DC and RF voltages only an ion with a certain mass to charge m/z ratio can pass through the mass filter and hit the detector, all the others ions will have unstable trajectories and collide with the rods. Thus, a mass spectrum can be obtained when the ions passing through the quadrupole are monitored as the applied ratio of DC and RF voltages is changing.

Although quadrupole mass spectrometers are convenient and easy to use, the resolution of the quadrupole mass filter is not sufficient to separate the ions with the same nominal m/z value.

Sector field ICP-MS spectrometers (ICP-SFMS) [95, 96] use magnetic and electric fields to separate the ions with different m/z values. The radius of the circular trajectory of an ion in the magnetic field depends on m/z and initial kinetic energy of the ion. Compared to the quadrupole mass spectrometers ($m/\Delta m < 300$), ICP-SFMS instruments provide much higher mass resolution ($m/\Delta m$ ~300-10000), allowing separation of the overlapped interferences. However, due to implementation of big magnets in their constructions, ICP-SFMS instruments are more expensive. Among other mass analyzers which can be applied to separate the ions according to their m/z ratio, time-of-flight (ToF) mass have to mentioned as well [97, 98]. The advances in the development of other alternative mass analyzers are presented in a recent review of G. M. Hieftje [99].

After the ion with a given m/z passes through a mass filter it is being counted with the detection system. ELAN 6000 ICP-QMS implements a dual-mode secondary electron multiplier as a detector. The detector in ELAN 6000 belongs to the discrete-dynode multiplier type. It consists of 22 discrete dynodes; when the ion hits the metal oxide film of the dynode it liberates secondary electrons. The electron optics of the detector accelerates these secondary electrons to the next dynode surface. The process is consequently repeated. Secondary electrons are being counted at the end of the detector [78]. ICP-SFMS instruments work with the similar detector system.

Dual mode means that at low signals pulse mode counting is used, where each ion corresponds to one electric pulse. At high signal levels, the analogue counting mode is implemented, measuring the current after amplification. Combining the pulse and analogue modes in one detector allows to extend the linear dynamic range of the ICP-MS instrument up to 8-9 orders of magnitude [100].

1.6.7. Interferences in ICP-MS.

Main analytical challenges in the ICP-MS analysis are the interferences of different nature [101]. All interferences in ICP-MS method can be divided into two groups: a) spectral interferences; b) non-spectral interferences. Among *spectral interferences* isobaric overlaps, double charged and polyatomic interferences can be distinguished [102]. *Non-spectral interferences* are mainly caused by matrix from concomitant species [103, 104]. Various strategies can be applied both during sample preparation procedure or ICP-MS operating itself to overcome the negative influence of indicated overlaps. Spectral interferences may be resolved using the following strategies: a) use of alternative masses; b) use of a high resolution mass spectrometer [105]; c) use of a mathematical interelement correction [106-109]. Concerning the non-spectral interferences the most common strategies include: a) probe dilution; b) separation of the sample matrix before the ICP-MS analysis [110-113]; c) matrix matched calibration and d) use of an internal standard [114].

In ICP-MS analysis of corrosion probes, non-spectral interferences are the most severe, due to the high concentration of alt matrix in liquid probes. Usually 0.1 M – 1 M NaCl solutions are used for corrosion experiments. Each strategy of interferences elimination has its advantages, but also restrictions and limits exist. The use of alternative masses helps to avoid isobaric and polyatomic interferences. This strategy can be applied only if the analyzed element has more than one isotope. Probe dilution is one of the easiest ways to overcome the influence of the matrix effects. Simple dilution of the probe allows to avoid strong matrix suppression of the analytical signal, clogging of cones, *etc*. However, probe dilution can only be used if concentrations of the elements of interest in the solution are high. Unfortunately, very often one or two elements in the probe are present in much higher concentration than the rest of the investigated elements. In addition, every subsequent dilution of the probe leads inevitably to a higher risk of dilution errors and contamination. The use of the internal standard and the interelement correction are effective strategies to conquer matrix influence. However, when the interelement correction is used, one should pay a special attention to reliability of the correction coefficients determination [106-109]. Additionally, in *in situ* corrosion experiments internal standardization is not usually applicable because of the corrosion medium pH change, due to acid standardized element- solutions.

1.7. Scope of the PhD thesis.

The scope of the present PhD project is to develop a novel analytical hyphenated technique for a spatial- and time-resolved chemical and electrochemical characterization of local corrosion processes in various metal alloys. It should also become a valuable tool for corrosion characterization of novel materials like bulk metallic glasses.

Fig. 1.11 shows a schematic overview of the proposed novel analytical technique.

It consists of four integral parts:

1) Microflow-capillary system, which allows a locally resolved attack of the material with corrosion solution flow;

2) Flow injection introduction system;

3) ICP mass spectrometer;

4) Electrochemical control (potentiostat).

Introduction

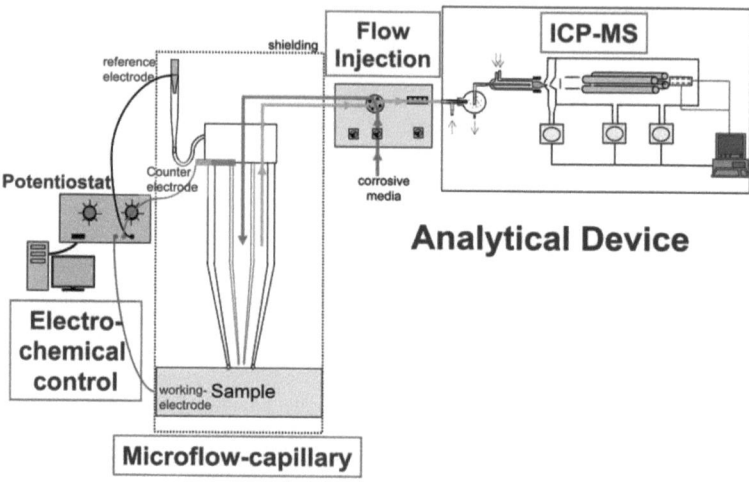

Fig. 1.11. Schematic overview of the novel analytical technique for local corrosion investigations (in the figure reference and counter electrodes are immersed in the corrosive solution).

Beside the construction steps, the technique should be analytically optimized and validated using independent methods common in corrosion research.

Microflow-capillary system.

The microflow-capillary system has to be developed to minimize the area of the corrosion attack (down to the µm-range) and to achieve continuous corrosive solution flow over the investigated sample. The minimization of the area of the corrosion attack is important, when local corrosion processes like influence of small intermetallics on the corrosion behaviour should be investigated or when the sample is not easily available on the market (Zr-bulk metallic glasses) and multiple corrosion investigation on a single sample should be performed.

Selection of the suitable material for the capillary represents a serious construction challenge. The selection needs to be performed with a special regard to low contamination levels originating from the capillary material to be suitable for trace and ultra-trace element chemical analysis. The cost issue is another important factor. The use of a new capillary for each experiment is mandatory due to memory effects. Therefore, a replacement of capillaries should be affordable. Development of a continuous solution flow for a capillary includes the development of an adjustable micro-pumping system with a pulse-free flow.

Flow injection introduction system (FI).

Online hyphenation of the microflow-capillary via the FI introduction system allows transient sampling and online corrosion sample introduction into the ICP-MS. Moreover, FI provides a high throughput of the analysis, minimized sample contamination risks and high reproducibility of probes injections. The absence of the sample handling and storage step in FI-ICP-MS is especially important in metal ultra-trace analysis, due to significantly reduced risks of the sample contamination. For the microflow-capillary set-up FI offers significant advantages over the conventional continuous flow sample introduction due to an excellent matrix tolerance even at a high level of total dissolved salt concentrations (*e.g.* 0.1-1 M NaCl) and a minimization of the required sample volumes (down to about 10 µl). This also improves detection limits and leads to a faster wash-out. However before the FI system can be coupled to ICP-MS its performance characteristics (sample uptake rate, volume of the FI loop, *etc.*) with respect to the analysis of the corrosion probes should be properly optimized.

Inductively coupled plasma mass spectrometry.

As it was explained above, ICP-MS provides simultaneous multi-element trace analysis with low detection limits, a broad linear range and high sensitivity. However, specific challenges related to the corrosion sample analysis, *e.g.* a high level of total dissolved solids (TDS) in corrosion probes or optimization of microflow characteristics, should be properly evaluated and treated before the technique can be applied for the corrosion investigation of real samples. Due to very small dissolution rates of secondary alloying elements, especially when only small spots are investigated to study local corrosion, another prerequisite is a minimized circulating liquid volume within the flow-capillary system. Thus, limited volume of the corrosive medium in the microflow-capillary represents a particular challenge for the novel technique. The total volume of the medium available for the analysis should be minimized to about 200 to 1000 µl as well as minimum sample aliquot volumes of 10 – 50 µl should be achieved. Therefore, a low flow sample introduction system (micronebulizer nebulizer and a low inner volume spray chamber) needs to be installed and optimized with a special regard to analysis of small liquid sample volumes (< 100 µl) for localized corrosion investigations.

Electrochemical control (3-electrode set-up).

The adaptation of the electrochemical control to the microflow-capillary FI-ICP-MS set-up opens new possibilities in corrosion studies by enabling simultaneous electrochemical and chemical element-specific data acquisition. Due to the hyphenation of potentiostat it is possible to control polarization of the investigated sample surface and induce specific corrosion processes. Moreover, it gives selective and independent information about corrosion initiation and the rate of corrosion processes taking place. However, the implementation of the electrochemical control is a challenging task.

It implies a selection of suitable electrode materials. Moreover, the dissolution and contamination background levels originating from the electrodes leaching have to be minimized. Hence, a careful evaluation of the electrodes by leach-out testing needs to be performed to select suitable electrode materials. Another critical task in the implementation of the electrochemical control is the minimization of the electrostatic noises which are critical when very low current densities are detected. A main source of different electrostatic noises is the solution circulation in the flow-capillary and the operation of FI system (peristaltic pumps, valve switching, etc.).

Validation and application of the technique.

The new microflow-capillary FI-ICP-MS technique with electrochemical control has to be validated using independent analytical techniques, *e.g.* electrochemical measurements, independent batch immersion tests and surface analytical techniques (SEM-EDX, *etc.*). Within the scope of the present PhD thesis the novel analytical technique is to be applied to the corrosion investigation of various materials, which are described in the following paragraph.

A. Commercially relevant, complex Al alloys which contain reactive intermetallic phases.

Due to its low weight, the use of Al alloys in transportation industry (automotive and airplane technology) is constantly growing [115]. In order to meet desired mechanical properties, secondary alloying elements such as Cu, Fe, Si, Mg, and Zn are added to improve the physical properties of the alloy. Since the added elements are often present not in the metal matrix, but in small intermetallic inclusions, they can accelerate the corrosion processes due to the formation of

Introduction

microgalvanic coupling with the aluminium matrix. Therefore, investigation of element-specific corrosion mechanisms for Al alloys is an important issue in corrosion research to improve the Al materials and estimate their life time and durability.

B. New amorphous materials, i.e. Zr-bulk metallic glasses.

The development of new amorphous metals or quasi-crystalline materials is of increasing interest for various industrial and medical applications. The properties of amorphous materials differs from those of crystalline metals and are characterized by outstanding hardness as well as high elastic formability and tensile strength [116, 117]. However, their corrosion behaviour is not well studied so far. Since bulk metallic glasses (*e.g.* Zr-BMGs) are proposed for medical applications, the investigation of their element-specific dissolution behaviour is of a special interest [118, 119].

2. Development of the microflow-capillary system. Offline feasibility corrosion analysis with ICP-MS.

(partly published in: N. Homazava, A. Ulrich, M. Trottmann, U. Krähenbühl, Micro-capillary system coupled to ICP-MS as a novel technique for investigation of micro-corrosion processes, Journal of Analytical Atomic Spectrometry 22 (2007) 1122–1130 [120].)

2.1. Overview.

The Chapter 2 describes the development of a hardware microflow-capillary system in combination with ICP-MS as a first step in the construction of the future novel analytical technique for element-specific time-resolved *in situ* characterization of localized corrosion processes. The development implies the construction of a suitable microflow-capillary set-up which allows a locally resolved attack of the material with corrosive medium flow, and subsequent introduction of this medium into an ICP-MS. Aspects in the analytical optimization of the system and validation by independent methods, *e.g.* SEM-EDX analysis, are discussed.

In this Chapter, the combination of microflow-capillary set-up with offline ICP-MS analysis afterwards was applied for the investigation of element-specific corrosion processes of several Al alloys (AA 1050, AA 5050 and AA 5754), commonly used in the automotive construction. The detailed element-resolved corrosion behaviour of AA 5754 was studied in 0.1M NaCl and 0.1M HCl. The data achieved with ICP-MS analysis is validated by a comparison to SEM-EDX analysis performed before and after corrosion experiment. Influencing factors such as exposure time and pH of the corrosive solution on elemental dissolution rates were studied with both techniques.

2.2. Experimental.

2.2.1. ICP-MS instrumentation and parameters.

Measurements were performed using two types of ICP-MS instrument: a quadrupole ICP-MS (ICP-QMS) ELAN 6000 (Perkin Elmer/Sciex) and a double focusing sector field ICP-MS

(ICP-SFMS) ELEMENT II (Thermo Fisher Scientific). The quadrupole ICP-MS was equipped with a concentric K-style Meinhard nebulizer with an uptake rate around 0.75 ml min^{-1} and a glass cyclonic spray chamber (Glass Expansion) to avoid memory effects and ensure a quick wash-out. The measuring times were optimized and finally set to: 25 sweeps per reading, 1 reading per replicate and 3 replicates. The dwell time was set to 30 ms for main elements (*e.g.*, Al, Mg) and 100 ms for ultratrace elements (*e.g.*, Cu, Cr Mn). The dual detector calibration was well adjusted including the elements of interest. The ICP-SFMS was equipped with a Sea Spray concentric nebuliser (Glass Expansion) with an uptake rate of about 0.8 ml min^{-1} and a glass cyclonic spray chamber (Glass Expansion). The instrument was operated in the medium mass resolution mode ($\Delta m/m$ = 4000) for all measurements. Both instruments were operated under hot plasma conditions; details are listed in Table 4.

Table 4. ICP-MS and ICP-SFMS operating conditions

ICP-MS Instrument	**ELAN 6000**	**ELEMENT II**
Plasma parameters		
Rf Power	1100 W	1250 W
Coolant gas flow-rate	15 L min^{-1}	16 L min^{-1}
Auxiliary gas flow-rate	1 L min^{-1}	0.85 L min^{-1}
Nebuliser gas flow-rate	0.92 L min^{-1}	0.96 L min^{-1}
Ion-sampling parameters		
Sampling and skimmer cones	Nickel	Nickel

The general idea of the novel technique is its applicability both for scientific and industrial research. ICP-QMS is more widely spread than ICP-SFMS. Moreover, the later online transient introduction *via* flow injection system requires an extremely fast data acquisition for multielement analysis as offered by ICP-QMS. Thus, ICP-SFMS was mainly used for comparison and confirmation of the applicability and efficiency of the developed analysis method in quadrupole technique. Both instruments provided comparable results. However, lower detection limits could be achieved for iron with ICP-SFMS instrument, since ^{56}Fe, the isotope of highest relative abundance, is accessible for direct determination under hot plasma conditions.

2.2.2. Scanning electron microscopy coupled with energy dispersive X-ray analysis (SEM-EDX).

Surface analytical technique SEM-EDX was used as an independent reference method. The surface microstructure before and after experimental tests was studied using an optical microscope (Zeiss-Axiovert 100A) and SEM (LEO 1455) equipped with EDX facility. EDX analysis was carried out using an Oxford INCA Energy 200 Instrument system during SEM examinations. Back-scattered and secondary electron images were obtained with 20 kV electron beam energy. Due to the localized nature of the corrosion attack in Al alloys SEM-EDX microstructural characterization was mainly focused on intermetallic particles as cathodic and anodic sites of the corrosion.

2.2.3. Materials and chemicals.

Materials used in the experiments were market relevant and commercially available Al wrought alloys. The chemical composition of the alloys is presented in Table 5. Samples with a size of 30 × 25 mm were cut from the as-received alloy sheet. Since surface roughness has a huge influence on corrosion processes in Al alloys [121], all samples were embedded in graphite and the sample surface was prepared by mechanical grinding with SiC papers down to 4000 grit followed by polishing to mirror quality with diamond paste down to 0.25 µm. Finally, the surface was ultrasonically cleaned with absolute ethanol (99.8 %, pro analysis, Merck, Darmstadt, Germany) to remove polishing residuals and dried at ambient air. The samples were not exposed to water during the grinding and polishing procedure to prevent selective dissolution of Mg [122]; instead, the surface of the samples was wet ground and polished with ethanol. The quality of the polished surface was checked with an optical microscope to ensure that no deep scratches or sites of local corrosion were present. To ensure the formation of the passivation oxide layer, the samples were stored in ambient air at least overnight before further corrosion investigations.

Table 5. Chemical composition (wt. %) of Al alloys.

Alloy	Mg	Si	Fe	Mn	Cu	Cr	Zn	Ti
AA 1050	0.004	0.09	0.31	–	0.04	0.002	0.003	0.01
AA 5050	1.31	0.15	0.39	0.26	0.10	–	0.05	–
AA 5754	2.83	0.21	0.30	0.23	0.05	0.02	0.01	0.01

The corrosion tests were performed in two different corrosive solutions at room temperature. The first medium was an aerated 0.1 M NaCl aqueous solution in 18.2 MΩ cm ultra-pure water, prepared by Milli-Q Gradient A10 supply system (Millipore, Bedford, MA, USA).

The sodium chloride was suprapur grade (99.99 %, Merck, Darmstadt, Germany). The pH value of the solution was 6.0. The second corrosive medium was an ultrapur 0.1 M HCl aqueous solution prepared by dilution of 30 % concentrated ultrapur HCl (Merck, Darmstadt, Germany) with pH 1.0 of the final solution. Exposure time varied from 5 min to 3 hours. The dissolution behaviour of Al alloys was investigated by means of ICP-MS method. The elemental concentrations in the corrosive solution were calculated as a function of impact time in corrosive media.

2.2.4. Sample preparation for ICP-MS analysis.

The exposition areas of the samples for the corrosion investigations had diameters of 1000 µm and 600 µm. After different specified impact time, the corrosive solution was quantitatively transferred into a pre-cleaned polypropylene tube. Samples used for ICP-MS analysis were prepared by diluting the solutions with ultrapur 1 % HNO_3 (Merck, Darmstadt, Germany) to the final volume of 5 ml for 0.1 M NaCl (pH 6.0) and final volume of 10 ml for 0.1 M HCl (pH 1.0). The solutions were spiked to 10 µg L^{-1} with Rh internal standard solution and analyzed by ICP-QMS and ICP-SFMS.

Multielement standard solutions were prepared by serial dilution of the 1 mg L^{-1} Merck IV multielement stock solution obtained from Merck (Darmstadt, Germany) with 1 % HNO_3 to concentration of 0.1, 0.5, 1, 5, 10 and 25 µg L^{-1}.

2.3. Results and discussion.

2.3.1. Construction of the microflow-capillary set-up.

A novel microflow-capillary system was constructed for the locally and element-resolved investigation of corrosion processes. Fig. 2.1 shows an overview of the built set-up. The sample, the microflow-capillary system positioned orthogonally to the sample and the peristaltic pump incorporated for continuous circulation of the corrosive medium are the main integral parts.

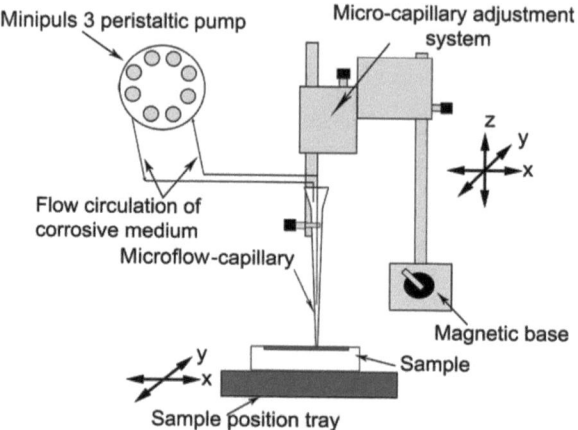

Fig. 2.1. Microflow-capillary set-up for element-specific investigation of corrosion processes

Several preliminary studies were necessary to perform prior to the construction of the above described complex set-up. As a first feasibility study, offline batch tests regarding a possible downscaling of the exposed area of the sample were carried out.

In these tests defined surface areas of the Al alloy sample were attacked by single droplets of 25 µl corrosive medium. The wetted surface area was about 5 mm in diameter (~ 0.2 cm^2 area affected). During exposure the alloy sample was posed on a plastic base in a closed vessel that was filled with a few millimetres deionised water to minimize droplet volatilisation (Fig. 2.2A). The influence of various experimental factors, such as corrosive medium type, pH of the medium and impact time was investigated. The results of these batch tests revealed that for the most Al alloys studied the concentrations of the main alloying elements like Al and Mg in the corrosive solution lay in the range of 1-10 mg L^{-1}. Even lower concentrated alloying metals could be detected in appropriate amounts. This finding confirmed the feasibility of the novel set-up construction with the reduced sample surface area exposed [123].

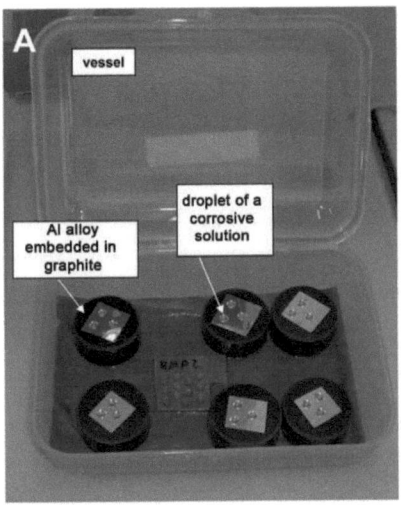 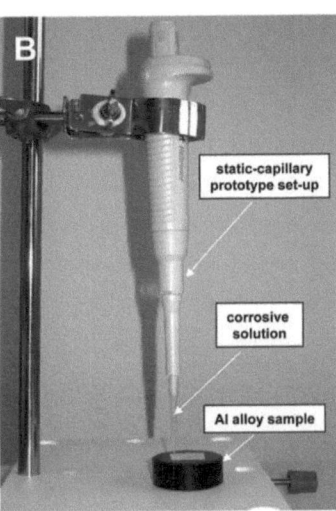

Fig. 2.2. A. Feasibility batch immersion tests; B. First static-capillary prototype set-up.

First, a prototype of the currently constructed set-up was built. Capillaries with two different opening sizes 1000 µm and 600 µm were tested to minimize the exposed area of the sample (Fig. 2.2 B). The influence of the decrease of the exposed area size on the dissolution rate is important for establishing the minimum capillary area size, which can be used in the microflow-capillary set-up.

The selection of a suitable material for a capillary represented a first construction challenge. A glass micro-capillary with silicone sealing proposed by T. Suter [19, 20] for a static electrochemical micro-capillary set-up is easy to handle and position on the sample surface. However, with respect to ultratrace analysis it is an unsuitable candidate due to several reasons. Leach-out analysis of glass and silicone materials resulted in the remarkable high background contamination for the elements of interest. Moreover, the material could absorb the elements released from the investigated alloy during the corrosion attack.

An alternative capillary material had to fulfil several requirements, such as cost efficiency, easy availability, easy handling and adjustment, self-sealing and low background contamination. Hence, polypropylene (PP) was chosen as a more appropriate material for the capillary. The softer material required no additional sealing. Exemplary results of the analytical testing of the PP-capillaries are presented in the following *Analytical Optimization* section.

The PP-capillary was filled with 0.1 M NaCl corrosive medium and positioned orthogonally to the sample surface. Fig. 2.3 presents the concentrations of Al and Mg in the corrosive solution after 3 hours of the corrosion attack. Detection limits (DLs) of ICP-MS analysis were calculated according to 3-Sigma-method as three times the standard deviation of 5 blank solutions. For comparability, all determined element concentrations as well as the given detection limits were calculated for undiluted corrosion medium. The Fig. 2.3 represents method related detection limits taking into account a 40-fold dilution factor.

The reduction of the capillary size from 1000 µm to 600 µm causes a drop in Al and Mg amounts released into corrosive medium for all Al alloys studied. The dissolution rates of Al and Mg for 600 µm capillary are on average 40-60 % of those for 1000 µm capillary. The results of elemental dissolution rates show a dependence of the absolute amount of element dissolved during corrosion attack on the size of the area affected. So far achievable detection limits shown in the same Fig. 2.3 confirm the possibility of the further decrease of a capillary opening size down to 250 µm at least.

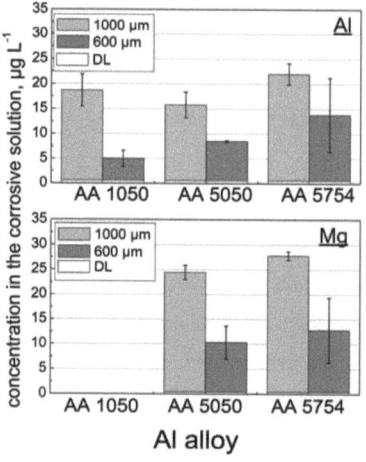

Fig. 2.3. Static capillary (1000 µm and 600 µm opening diameters) tests. Elemental dissolution rates from Al alloys in 0.1 M NaCl corrosive medium.

However, further strategies to minimize background levels and contamination risks should be studied to enable the detection of decreased elemental release rates also for low concentrated alloying elements. Although the static capillary tests provided completely new element-specific quantitative data on elemental dissolution rates for different Al alloys, this prototype set-up suffered from some disadvantages and limitations. The insufficient precision in the capillary positioning on the sample led to increased relative standard deviations (RSDs) 25-50 % of the results (Fig. 2.3). Additionally, the lack of the circulation of corrosive medium in the system limited the experimental set conditions by static tests only. Thus, a new microflow-capillary set-up shown in Fig. 2.1 was constructed to overcome the mentioned disadvantages.

To ensure a precise adjustment of the new set-up, the microflow-capillary system was mounted into a special path of a manual XYZ-axis micromanipulator (World Precision Instruments, Sarasota, FL, USA). The micromanipulator was fixed on a magnetic stand and mounted to a magnetically steel base with dimensions of 30.5 × 61.0 cm to provide stable support. Vernier scales of the manipulator permit readings to 0.1 mm and X-axis fine control permits 10 µm readings, thus allowing a precise positioning of the capillary on the surface of the sample.

The sample was mounted on a XY-axis stage (Misumi Europa GmbH, Schwalbach, Germany) orthogonally to the capillary. The stage is characterized by 10 µm minimum reading and additionally fitted on a magnetic base. Thus, the capability to control both XYZ-axis movement of the capillary and XY-axis movement of the sample guarantee an exact and reproducible alignment of the capillary and the sample.

A Gilson (Villiers Le Bel, France) Minipuls 3 peristaltic pump was used to assure a contamination minimized and well adjustable flow of the corrosive medium within the microflow-capillary set-up. The total volume of the corrosive medium used was optimized to 250 µl. The media flow control allows an adjustment of the internal cycling flux between 50 µl min^{-1} and 1000 µl min^{-1}. In current experimental tests the internal cycling flux in the system was optimized and finally set to 500 µl min^{-1} to ensure a laminar flow of the solution and to avoid the formation of air bubbles inside the pumping tubes. The tubing material used in the peristaltic pump was made of polyvinylchloride (PVC) with internal diameter of 0.89 mm (Ismatec, Switzerland).

2.3.2. Analytical optimization of the microflow-capillary set-up.

Since concentrations of elements during static capillary were determined in a low µg L^{-1} range, a special attention was paid to possible contamination sources. PP-capillaries and PP-tubes could be an origin for contamination, *e.g.*, due to manufacturing residuals, impurities or additives in the polymer [124]. Thus, PP-capillaries and -tubes used for sample preparation or experimental tests were preliminary subjected to a specially developed pre-cleaning procedure. The optimization resulted in the following final pre-cleaning procedure.

First, capillaries and tubes were rinsed with 18.2 MΩ cm ultra-pure water, then cleaned for 3 minutes with suprapur 63 % HNO_3 and thoroughly rinsed with ultra-pure water once again. After this, the tubes were immersed for 3 hours in an aqueous 1:10 HNO_3 solution. Finally, the vessels were leached in 1 % ultrapur HNO_3 overnight and rinsed several times with ultra-pure water.

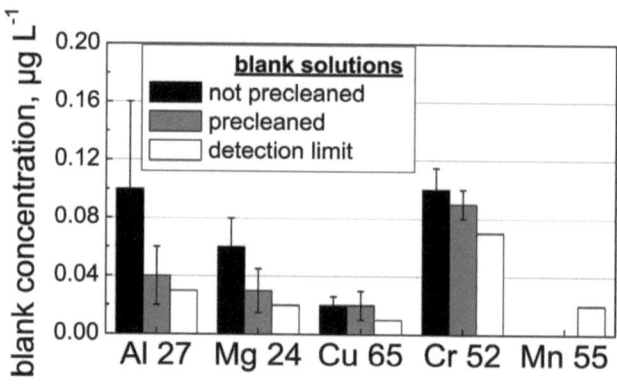

Fig. 2.4. Elemental concentrations in blank solutions before and after capillary pre-cleaning procedure (in 0.1 M NaCl, 20-fold dilution factor).

After the cleaning the PP-capillaries and -tubes were filled with ultra-pure water and stored in a closed hood until use. The efficiency of the cleaning procedure was controlled by analysis of blank solutions before and after cleaning procedure using ICP-MS (Fig. 2.4).

Beside minimization of contamination risks, strategies for analysis of high salt content solutions had to be investigated. With respect to a minimization of non-spectral interferences (*e.g.*, change in viscosity and nebulisation properties, signal depression due to electron density change in the plasma *etc.*) and spectral interferences (*e.g.*, formation of Na or Cl related polyatomic interferences), it is recommended to limit the amount of total dissolves salts in a liquid probe to about 1 % total dissolved salt content for convectional sample introduction ICP-MS systems. Thus, the degree of interferences has to be assessed. Beside a careful analyte ion selection for all elements of interest, the application of internal standardization, matrix matching versus dilution strategies, careful adjustment of dual detection calibration including all analytes and interfering matrix elements as well as custom resolution adjustment for specific elements have been evaluated.

The potential spectral overlaps for Al alloys corrosion studies in NaCl medium are listed in Table 6. Finally, a 40-fold dilution was used to overcome non-spectral signal suppression and minimize polyatomic spectral interferences. Additionally, ICP-MS analysis in the medium resolution mode using a magnetic sector field ICP-SFMS ELEMENT II was performed for the secondary alloying elements (Fe, Cr, Mn and Cu) which are potentially interfered in quadrupole ICP-MS.

Table 6. Possible interferences for analyte ions in NaCl matrix.

Analyte ion	Relative abundance	Interferences	Mass resolution required
$^{52}Cr^+$	83.79	$^{35}Cl^{16}O^1H^+$	1672
		$^{35}Cl^{17}O^+$	1892
		$^{37}Cl^{15}N^+$	2038
$^{53}Cr^+$	9.50	$^{37}Cl^{16}O^+$	2626
		$^{35}Cl^{17}O^1H^+$	1507
$^{55}Mn^+$	100	$^{37}Cl^{18}O^+$	2035
$^{63}Cu^+$	69.17	$^{40}Ar^{23}Na^+$	2792

2.3.3. Application of the offline microflow-capillary set-up for the investigation of micro-corrosion processes in Al alloy 5754.

Alloy microstructure.

Al alloy 5754 is an Al-Mg alloy and is typically used in the automotive industry. Fig. 2.5A shows optical and scanning electron microscopic images of the final polished surface of an AA 5754 alloy sample. Optical microscopic observations confirmed a uniform distribution of second phase particles throughout the alloy. Two main types of intermetallics, *i.e.*, Al(Fe,Mn) and Mg_2Si, are easily distinguished on the SEM micrograph. Similar IMPs were identified in other Al-Mg and Al-Mg-Si alloys [125, 126]. Particles rich in iron and manganese are visible on the SEM micrograph in light tone and magnesium-silicon particles in dark tone.

EDX analysis performed on ten particles of each type confirmed the chemical composition of the intermetallics. Fig. 2.5B shows exemplary SEM images of single Mg_2Si and $Al(Fe,Mn)$ particles and corresponding EDX spectra.

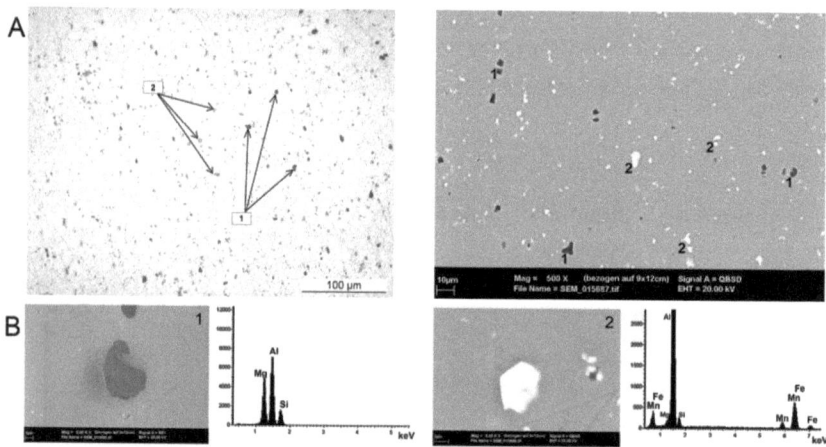

Fig. 2.5. A. Optical and SEM images of the polished AA 5754 surface; B. SEM-EDX micrographs of the single intermetallic particles.

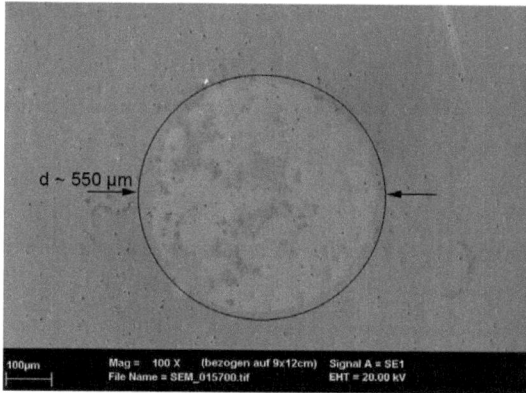

Fig. 2.6. SEM image of the alloy surface after the immersion in 0.1 M NaCl for 30 min. The circle with a diameter of about 550 µm points the spot, where the micro-capillary was placed.

Element-specific corrosion processes.

In order to study elemental dissolution rates of AA 5754, the polished sample surface was exposed to 0.1 M NaCl and 0.1 M HCl corrosive solutions. 600 μm opening size of the capillary was used in the current set-up. Fig. 2.6 demonstrates a SEM image of the sample surface after corrosion in 0.1 M NaCl for 30 min; the circle points the spot where the capillary with the corrosive solution was placed.

ICP-MS analysis of the corrosive solutions was applied to provide element-resolved data on time-dependent localized corrosion processes in AA 5754.

Table 7 lists the determined detection limits obtained in μg L^{-1} for measurements performed using a quadrupole ICP-MS ELAN 6000 and ICP-SFMS ELEMENT II. To relate the results to the surface area exposed to the corrosion attack, equivalent detection limits in μg cm^{-2} are given.

Table 7. ICP-QMS and ICP-SFMS detection limits (3-sigma -method) for analyte ions, in μg L^{-1} and converted to μg cm^{-2}.

Analyte ion	Detection limits, μg L^{-1}		Equivalent detection limits, μg cm^{-2}	
	ICP-QMS	ICP-SFMS	ICP-QMS	ICP-SFMS
^{27}Al$^+$	0.03	-	0.06	-
^{24}Mg$^+$	0.02	-	0.04	-
^{65}Cu$^+$	0.01	0.0008	0.01	0.0014
^{52}Cr$^+$	0.07	0.0004	0.13	0.0007
^{55}Mn$^+$	0.02	0.0001	0.04	0.0002
^{56}Fe$^+$	-	0.006	-	0.01

Al dissolution.

The results of time depending Al dissolution from AA 5754 after corrosion attack of 0.1 M NaCl and 0.1 M HCl are shown in Fig. 2.7A. The concentrations of Al released from the alloy were calculated for undiluted corrosive solutions and converted from μg L^{-1} concentrations to μg cm^{-2} based on the exposed area. The estimated RSDs varied from 7 to 22 % for the concentrations measured in 0.1 M NaCl solution and from 13 to 37 % for 0.1 M HCl solution.

The observed increase of aluminium concentration in the solution with increasing impact time for both neutral and acidic media can be explained by constant rate of the corrosion attack with time. The data also indicate a significant increase of Al dissolution with decreasing pH due to the oxide layer instability.

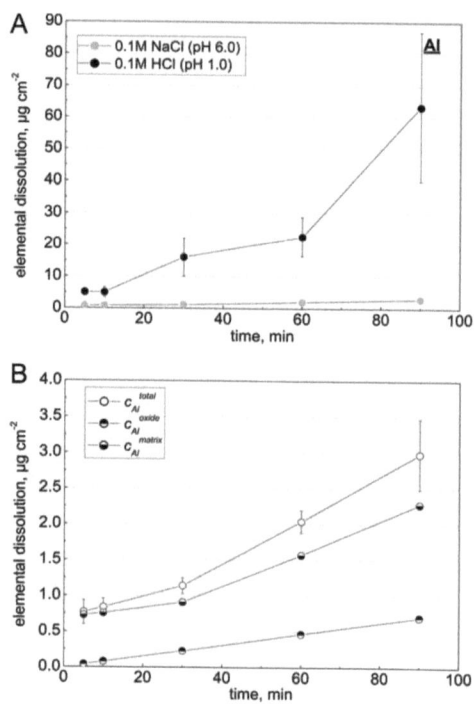

Fig. 2.7. A. Aluminium dissolution from AA 5754 in 0.1 M NaCl and 0.1 M HCl corrosive media; B. Aluminium dissolution from AA 5754 as a sum of Al dissolution from the oxide layer and Al matrix in 0.1M NaCl

The amount of Al dissolved from AA 5754 after 5 min exposure time in 0.1 M HCl is approximately 5 times higher than in 0.1 M NaCl and a static increase of Al dissolution is observed for all distinct intervals within the total impact time of 90 min. The Al release from AA 5754 into 0.1 M HCl is about 5 to 20 times higher then into 0.1 M NaCl.

This finding is in agreement with results of A. Kolics *et al.* [64], who also reported a pH influence on dissolution of aluminium oxide in acidic (pH < 4.0) and alkaline (pH > 10.0) media using ICP-OES method. However, the detection limits achievable by ICP-OES do not allow determinations of aluminium dissolution rates in media with neutral pH. The novel set-up based on ICP-MS method is characterized by much lower detection limits and permits quantitative analysis of localized dissolution processes both in neutral and acidic media.

Pitting corrosion of Al alloys is influenced both by the stability of the oxide layer and by the presence of intermetallic compounds which may behave anodically or cathodically relatively to the matrix. Due to the galvanic coupling between the IMPs and the Al matrix, the anodic reaction of Al dissolution occurs mainly on the matrix, which surrounds the cathodic sites of the corrosion, *i.e.*, Al(Fe,Mn) intermetallics [15]. Hence, the aluminium concentration in the solution can be expressed as the sum of the concentrations of aluminium released from the oxide film and aluminium released from the matrix of AA 5754 after the local breakdown of the oxide layer:

$$c_{Al}^{total} = c_{Al}^{oxide} + c_{Al}^{matrix} \qquad (2.1)$$

The contribution of Al originated from the oxide layer c_{Al}^{oxide} and the matrix c_{Al}^{matrix} can be calculated based on the dissolution rate $R_{dis} \sim 2.4 \times 10^{-12}$ mol cm^{-2} s^{-1} of the Al$_2$O$_3$ passive film on pure Al in neutral solutions (Fig. 2.7B) [127]. It can be assumed that the real value of c_{Al}^{oxide} can be slightly different for AA 5754 than for pure Al due to the different oxide layer structures. However, from the curves behaviour in Fig. 2.7B it can be concluded that the process of oxide film dissolution results in a significant contribution on the total amount of Al dissolved.

The slope angle of the Al dissolution curve in neutral medium is much smaller than in the acidic corrosive solution. The noticeable change can be explained by difference in Al solubility at different pHs. On one hand, the local concentration of Al ions at the oxide film/solution interface is assumed to reach its maximum at neutral pH, resulting in Al(OH)$_3$ precipitation on the alloy surface. On the other hand, the oxide layer is no longer stable in 0.1 M HCl. Low pH of the solution hinders Al^{3+} from precipitation due to higher solubility of Al species in acidic media, resulting in a higher slope angle of the Al dissolution curve.

Mg dissolution.

Fig. 2.8A shows Mg dissolution from AA 5754 in 0.1 M NaCl and 0.1 M HCl solution. The general trend of increasing dissolution rates depending on the exposure time for Mg is similar to that of Al.

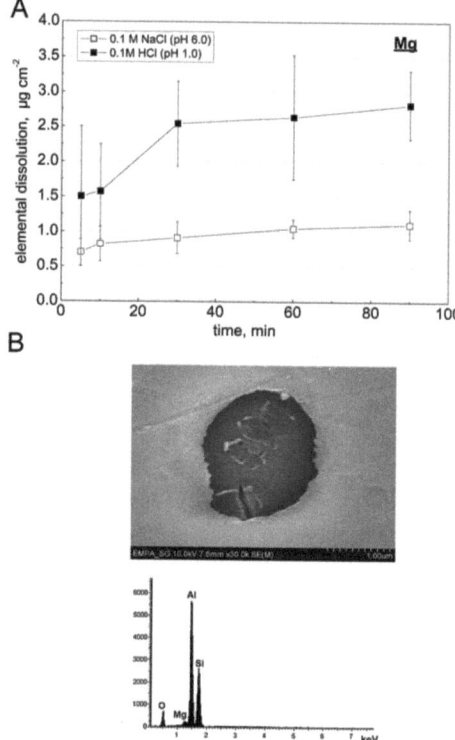

Fig. 2.8. A. Magnesium dissolution from AA 5754 in 0.1 M NaCl and 0.1 M HCl corrosive media; B. SEM micrograph of Mg_2Si intermetallic and EDX spectrum acquired from it after 60 minutes of exposure in 0.1M NaCl.

Magnesium shows also higher dissolution rates in acidic medium in comparison to neutral. However, the exact behaviour is somewhat different. While Al showed a stable increase of the dissolution rate with the exposure time, the dissolution rate of Mg reaches a constant level after a primary increase. The concentration of Mg dissolving into the corrosive solution can be expressed as the sum of concentrations of Mg selectively dissolving from Mg$_2$Si particles, Mg dissolving from the oxide layer and Mg concomitantly dissolving from the Al matrix:

$$c_{Mg}^{total} = c_{Mg}^{IMPs} + c_{Mg}^{oxide} + c_{Mg}^{matrix} \qquad (2.2)$$

EDX spectra acquired from the matrix of AA 5754 showed the Mg content in the Al matrix to be about 3 at %. According to the Al dissolution rates, the calculated contribution of c_{Mg}^{matrix} into c_{Mg}^{total} does not significantly influence the behaviour of experimental curves of Mg dissolution. The c_{Mg}^{oxide} and c_{Mg}^{IMPs} signals, however, can not be distinguished due to the absence of data on dissolution rates of Mg from Al alloys oxide layer in the literature. Hence, the experimental curves obtained for Mg dissolution at neutral and acidic pH characterize simultaneously the release of Mg both from the oxide layer and from Mg$_2$Si intermetallic compounds. However, it can be assumed that the contribution of c_{Mg}^{IMPs} into the total amount of Mg dissolved is notably higher than c_{Mg}^{oxide} due to the reasons discussed further on.

The Mg release from AA 5754 at pH 1.0 reveals two regions with different slopes. The first region with an exposure time up to about 30 min is characterized by a remarkable increase of Mg dissolution. The second region of the curve, starting from 30 min, can be described as a quasi-plateau state and shows a significantly lower increase of the Mg dissolution into the corrosive medium expressed by only a slight change from 2.5 µg cm^{-2} after 30 min to 2.8 µg cm^{-2} after 90 min of exposure. The sudden change in the dissolution behaviour can be explained by the selective dissolution of Mg from Mg$_2$Si intermetallics.

Mg$_2$Si intermetallics described by corrosion potential E_{corr} = -1538 mV$_{SCE}$ (0.1 M NaCl, pH 6) [15] are typically anodic relative to the matrix. The lower potential leads to selective dissolution of Mg$_2$Si during the corrosion attack. This explains also the sudden drop of Mg dissolution rate after 30 min exposure time in 0.1 M HCl and reaching of a quasi-plateau state. At initial stages the selective dissolution of Mg from Mg$_2$Si particles occurs and, within 30 min exposure time, all Mg from inclusions is completely dissolved.

The same conclusions can be made for Mg dissolution at neutral pH, even if the two regions are less clear distinguishable. Fig. 2.8A indicates a small reduction in the dissolution rate after approximately 45 min of exposure in NaCl. The dissolution of Mg from particles is confirmed by SEM-EDX analysis of the Mg$_2$Si particles after exposure in NaCl solution for 60 min (Fig. 2.8B). EDX acquired after the corrosion attack clearly indicates magnesium dissolution by significantly reduced Mg signal in the spectrum compared to EDX spectrum before attack.

The slope angles of the Mg release into NaCl and HCl solutions at initial stages resemble those of Al on Fig. 2.7A. The low pH of HCl solution prevents Mg^{2+} from precipitating resulting in a higher slope angle of Mg dissolution curve.

Secondary elements dissolution.

One of the main advantages of the new analytical technique is the possibility to study simultaneously not only the dissolution behaviour of the main alloying elements such as Al and Mg but also of secondary elements such as Fe or Mn, which are present in the alloy in much smaller quantities. Secondary alloying elements such as Fe, Cr, Mn and Cu can be also released into the corrosive solution. The investigation of their corrosion dissolution behaviour is very interesting for the interpretation of possible corrosion mechanisms. For the here studied alloy, only Fe showed a detectable release into the solution, whereas lower concentrated elements such as Cr, Mn or Cu were not detected in the corrosive solution. To study Fe elemental release the corrosive solutions were investigated by ICP-SFMS.

Fe dissolution.

Fig. 2.9A describes the Fe dissolution behaviour as a function of exposure time in corrosive media. The Fe curves also showed an enhanced dissolution in acidic medium compared to neutral, following a similar pattern to that of Al and Mg dissolution graphs.

The enhancement of Fe release with increasing exposure time and decreasing pH value is observed. The release of Fe in acidic medium is, on average two times higher than in neutral. At the initial stages of AA 5754 localized corrosion, the alloy releases into 0.1 M NaCl solution 0.1 µg cm^{-2} of Fe after 5 min of the attack and the amount of dissolved iron reaches 0.4 µg cm^{-2} after 90 min. The acidic solution provokes the higher amount of Fe to be dissolved, giving a rise from 0.4 µg cm^{-2} after 5 min to 0.75 µg cm^{-2} after 90 min of the corrosion attack.

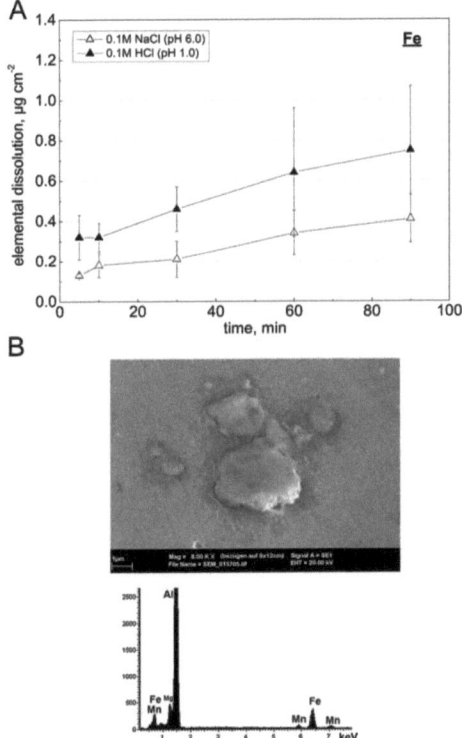

Fig. 2.9. A. Iron dissolution from AA 5754 in 0.1 M NaCl and 0.1 M HCl corrosive media; B. SEM micrograph of Al(Fe,Mn) intermetallic and EDX spectrum acquired from it after 30 minutes of exposure in 0.1M NaCl.

Since iron has a negligibly small solid solubility in the Al matrix, it is considered to be localized in Al(Fe,Mn) intermetallics which behave cathodic relative to the matrix. Anodic reaction on the adjacent matrix leads to the preferential Al dissolution around cathodic IMPs, resulting in pits formation.

Fig. 2.9B shows a SEM micrograph of Al(Fe,Mn) intermetallic and EDX spectrum of it after 30 min of exposure in 0.1 M NaCl. The image reveals the host matrix dissolution and the Fe dissolution at the edges of IMP, as confirmed by ICP-MS analysis of the corrosive solutions.

The possible precipitation of Al^{3+} generates a formation of H^+ ions:

$$Al^{3+} + 3H_2O \rightarrow Al(OH)_3 + 3H^+ \qquad (2.3)$$

Thus, Fe dissolution at the edges of intermetallics is assumed to be caused by the local acidification in the pits. This was also proposed by P. Schmutz and G.S. Frankel. [128, 129].

As shown in Fig. 2.9B, EDX analysis was not sensitive enough to detect the difference in spectra acquired from Al(Fe,Mn) IMPs in as-polished condition and after 30 min of the corrosion attack, while ICP-MS analysis provided quantitative data on time-dependent process of Fe dissolution.

2.4. Conclusions.

The results for the present offline microflow-capillary system with a subsequent sample introduction to ICP-MS and the comparison of the achieved data for real Al samples to SEM-EDX results confirmed the high efficiency of the offline set-up.

The microflow-capillary system allowed local corrosion attack of the investigated material with a defined spatial resolution. The stable pulse-free circulating flow of the corrosive solution within the capillary was achieved using the peristaltic pump.

Thus, the microflow-capillary system offline combined with ICP-MS provided new important information on investigations of localized corrosion processes. The main advantage compared to other methods is the availability of time-resolved and element-specific analysis for localized corrosion investigations. The established detection limits are at extremely low levels of about 0.01-0.06 $\mu g\ cm^{-2}$ which allow element-specific corrosion investigations not only for the main alloying elements but also a quantification of secondary alloying element release, *e.g.*, Fe.

Chapter 2

3. Online hyphenation of the microflow-capillary system to ICP-MS using flow injection sample introduction. – An application for *in situ* corrosion characterization of Al alloy 6111.

(partly published in: N. Homazava, A. Ulrich, U. Krähenbühl, Spatially and time-resolved element-specific in situ corrosion investigation with an online hyphenated microcapillary flow injection inductively coupled plasma mass spectrometry set-up, Spectrochimica Acta Part B 63 (2008) 777–783 [130].)

3.1. Overview.

Chapter 3 presents the next step in the technique development: an online hyphenation of the offline microflow-capillary set-up to the ICP-MS instrument using flow injection sample introduction system.

Flow injection is an appropriate way for transient sample introduction of µl-volumes into ICP-MS in *in situ* or *in vivo* experiments. Recently some applications of FI for *in situ* and *in vivo* analysis have been developed, *e.g.* implementation of flow injection for *in situ* analysis of Fe in hydrothermal environment [131], FI-ICP-MS analysis of leaching rocks with online determination of released elements [132], or *in vivo* trace elements determination in brain fluids of anesthetized rats [133, 134].

As compared to the previous offline set-up (described in Chapter 2), the new online FI-ICP-MS set-up should offer significant advantages in the corrosion research. The previous set-up enabled only a very limited amount of measurements per time unit. Investigations at different spots were required for time-resolved studies, because the whole solution in the capillary was needed for the analysis. Moreover, the special sample preparation procedure was required (*e.g.* dilution of the probes due to the high salt content of the probes).

The new online set-up allows a time resolved sampling of aliquots for *in situ* analysis at a single spot of the alloy, which is especially significant, when the dissolution processes at the initial stages of corrosion are studied. This means it enables real transient monitoring of corrosion processes at one point. The novel FI-ICP-MS set-up is also designed to tolerate high matrix of the probes. FI provides high throughput of the analysis, minimized sample contamination risks and high reproducibility of probes injections.

However, specific challenges related to the proposed technique, *e.g.* a high level of total dissolved solids in corrosion probes, optimization of microflow characteristics or a limited volume of the corrosion medium in the microflow-capillary set-up, should be properly evaluated and treated before the technique can be applied for the corrosion investigation of real samples. Thus, the goal of the present Chapter is an online hyphenation of the recently constructed microflow-capillary set-up to ICP-MS *via* flow injection system and a subsequent optimization of the technique.

The efficiency of the developed technique is proved by corrosion susceptibility analysis of a commercial Al alloy. Results of the corrosion experiments of the aluminium alloy AA 6111 are presented to demonstrate the influence of various factors such as exposure time and pH value of the corrosive medium on the element-specific dissolution rates of the alloy.

3.2. Experimental.

3.2.1. ICP-MS instrumentation.

The coupling of the microflow-capillary to ICP-MS was realized with a quadrupole ICP-MS ELAN 6000 (Perkin Elmer/Sciex) was used for all measurements. To minimize the total volume in the microflow-capillary down to 200-1000 µl and sample aliquots to 10-50 µl only, a special low flow sample introduction system (Micromist nebulizer and Cinnabar spray chamber) was installed. It was demonstrated in literature that Micromist nebulizer shows an efficient and accurate performance (low oxide and double charge species levels) at sample uptake rates < 100 µl min^{-1} [83, 86]. Moreover, Cinnabar spray chamber with a reduced internal volume of 20 cm^3 revealed significantly shorter wash-out times in comparison with a conventional cyclonic spray chamber (40 cm^3) [82, 85].

Thus, the instrument was equipped with a low flow nebulizer Micromist (Glass Expansion, Australia) operating at a sample uptake rate of 50 µl min^{-1} (MMN50). The performance of two spray chambers: Twister conventional glass cyclonic spray chamber (Glass Expansion, Australia) and mini-cyclonic Cinnabar spray chamber (Glass Expansion, Australia) was also evaluated. The volumes of the spray chambers were 40 cm^3 and 20 cm^3, respectively. Finally, Cinnabar spray chamber with a reduced inner volume was used for all measurements. The operating conditions of ELAN 6000 are listed in Table 8.

Table 8. ICP-MS operating conditions.

ICP-MS Instrument	ELAN 6000
Operating parameters	
Rf Power (W)	1100
Coolant gas flow-rate (L min^{-1})	15.00
Auxiliary gas flow-rate (L min^{-1})	1.00
Nebulizer gas flow-rate (L min^{-1})	1.06
Ion-sampling parameters	
Sampling and skimmer cones	Nickel
Data acquisition parameters	
Dwell time (ms)	50
Readings per replicate	150
Number of replicates	20
Analytes monitored	$^{27}Al^+$, $^{24}Mg^+$, $^{55}Mn^+$, $^{65}Cu^+$

3.2.2. Flow injection analysis system.

For transient sample introduction a FIAS-200 (Perkin Elmer/Sciex) operated under computer control of ELAN 6000 system software was used. The flow manifold consisted of two incorporated peristaltic pumps and a multi-port switching valve. To ensure low level contamination tubing made of PTFE with internal diameters 0.18 cm or 0.25 cm (VICI AG, Switzerland) was used in the flow manifold. Ferrules and connectors used in the flow manifold were also purchased from VICI AG (Switzerland).

The volume of the sample loop was optimized to minimum sample consumption and finally set to 20 µl and the sample uptake rate to 100 µl min^{-1}. An external Minipuls 3 peristaltic pump (Gilson, France) was used to pump the drain from the spray chamber.

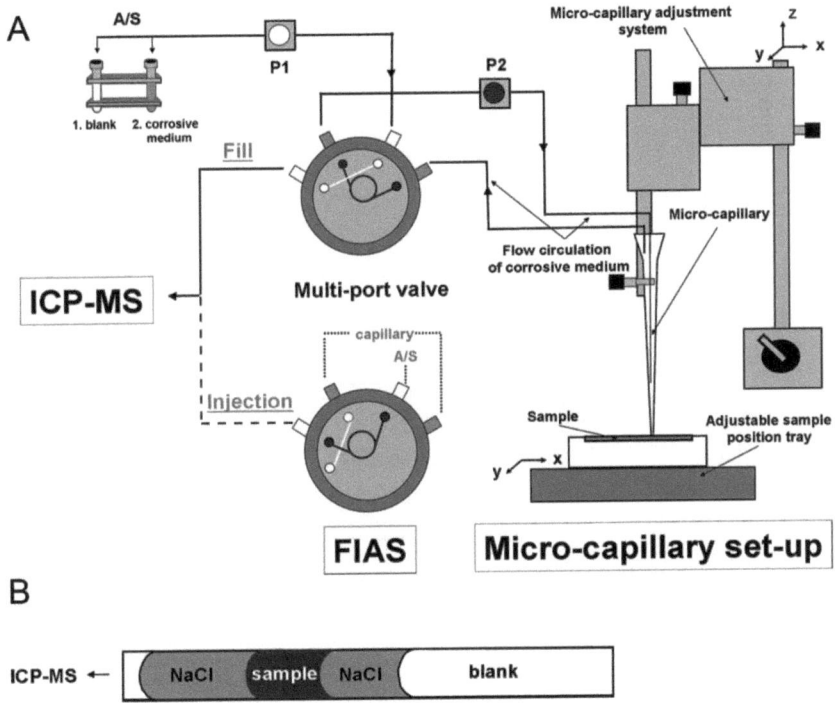

Fig. 3.1. A. Microflow-capillary set-up in online FI hyphenation with ICP-MS designed for *in situ* corrosion research; B. flow strategy of liquid sample introduction into ICP-MS.

A scheme of the microflow-capillary set-up in online hyphenation with FI-ICP-MS is shown in Fig. 3.1. A detailed description of the construction and development of the microflow-capillary set-up itself can be found in the previous Chapter 2. The parameters of FI program are listed in Table 9.

The corrosive medium was pumped via integrated peristaltic pump (P2) with a cycling flux of 500 µl min^{-1}. The flow, leading to ICP-MS, was pumped through the peristaltic pump P1 at a sample uptake rate of 100 µl min^{-1}. The volume of the corrosive medium in the capillary set-up was set to 250 µl. After a program defined time, the valve automatically turned from the position one to the position two and the sample loop, containing the corrosion probe, was injected from the loop into the flow stream and introduced to ICP-MS. At the same time the loop was filled with fresh NaCl medium and then transferred back to the capillary flow (the valve switched back).

Table 9. Finally used flow injection program.

Step	Read	Duration, s	P1, rpm	P2, rpm	Valve	A/S, position
Pre step		1	25	60	1	1 (1% HNO_3)
Step 1		71	25	60	1	2 (0.1 M NaCl)
Step 2		5	25	60	1	1 (1% HNO_3)
Step 3		8	100	0	2	1 (1% HNO_3)
Step 4	X	95	25	60	1	1 (1% HNO_3)
Step 5 x2		90	25	60	1	1 (1% HNO_3)

To avoid the error in the calculation of the metal amount released from the alloy a small dilution factor was taken into account during the calculations. Thus, the final amount of metal dissolved at each step was calculated as the sum of the actual measured metal concentration adding the amount which was probed in the previous sampling, using 20 µl sample loop.

Schematically, the order of the liquid probe introduction into ICP-MS instrument is represented in Fig. 3.1B. To ensure the best stability, FI program was so designed that a small amount of NaCl medium was introduced before and after the sample, containing the same medium as a matrix. This improves the instrument performance and stabilizes the signal intensities.

3.2.3. Data processing.

Raw data acquired in the intensity *vs.* time mode were exported to Origin 6.1G software (OriginLab Corporation, MA, USA) and smoothed with 11-point Savitzky-Golay moving window. Both peak height and peak area data were calculated using the same software. The background subtraction from the peak profile was systematically performed based on 5-baseline readings prior to the peak acquirement.

3.2.4. Materials and chemicals.

Material used for corrosion investigation was a commercial wrought aluminium alloy AA 6111, which is typically used in aerospace and automotive industries. The alloy contains the following alloying elements: Si (0.80% wt.), Fe (0.26% wt.), Cu (0.70% wt.), Mn (0.21% wt.),

Mg (0.61% wt.) and Cr (0.02% wt.). The alloy specimen with dimensions of 25 × 25 mm was embedded in graphite. Alloy sample surface was grinded with SiC paper down to 4000 grit, followed by polishing with a diamond paste down to 0.25 µm. It was shown that some alloying elements (e.g. Mg) dissolve in water during grinding and polishing procedures [122], thus ethanol was used instead. After the final polishing, the surface of the alloy was ultrasonically cleaned and examined with an optical microscope. To ensure the formation of the passivation oxide layer, the samples were stored in ambient air at least overnight before further corrosion investigations.

0.1 M NaCl solutions at three different values of pH (2.0, 4.0 and 6.0) were employed as corrosive media. Sodium chloride was of suprapur grade (99.99%, Merck, Germany). All solutions were prepared in 18.2 MΩ cm ultra-pure water (Milli-Q Gradient A10 supply system, Millipore, MA, USA); pHs of the solutions were adjusted by adding HCl (ultrapur, Merck, Germany).

Alloy specimens with an area of 0.28 mm^2 (the orifice of the microcapillary equal to 600 µm) were exposed to corrosive media during 2 h with FI-ICP-MS online monitoring of the multi-element release.

Due to the lack of suitable certified reference materials, the synthetic corrosion solution, containing 20 µg L^{-1} of Al, 10 µg L^{-1} of Mg, 1 µg L^{-1} of Cr, Cu, Mn and 10 µg L^{-1} of Rh (internal standard) in 0.1 M NaCl solution, was employed. The synthetic solution was prepared from single element stock solutions (1000 mg L^{-1}) of ICP-MS quality (Merck, Darmstadt, Germany). The optimization of the introduction system characteristics and flow injection parameters was carried out using this synthetic solution.

The calibration procedure was performed using matrix matched (0.1M NaCl) multi-element standard solutions (1 µg L^{-1}, 5 µg L^{-1}, 20 µg L^{-1} and 100 µg L^{-1}) prepared in 18.2 MΩ cm ultra-pure water (Milli-Q Gradient A10 supply system, Millipore, MA, USA) from 1000 mg L^{-1} multielement stock solution Merck IV (Merck, Germany).

3.3. Results and discussion.

3.3.1. Alternative sample introduction system.

A minimization of the microcapillary dimensions is required to implement local *in situ* corrosion analysis. Here, a microcapillary with a 600 µm orifice was used. Consequently, the volume of the corrosive medium circulating in the capillary system needs to be reduced according to the minimization of the microcapillary dimensions. Furthermore, a minimization of the medium volume is desirable to avoid an additional dilution and the very low concentrations of elements released from the alloy.

Hence, an alternative ICP-MS sample introduction system is needed, which enables low sample uptake rates (< 200 µl min^{-1}) and a reliable nebulization of corrosion samples with a high TDS content at the same time. In the present study an introduction system, consisting of a low-flow Micromist nebulizer and a Cinnabar spray chamber with the reduced internal volume was evaluated for ICP-MS analysis of small volume corrosion probes. Its performance was optimized in terms of nebulizer gas flow rate, Ba^{++}/Ba^{+} and CeO^{+}/Ce^{+} ratios, maximum signal intensities and optimum nebulization precision (relative standard deviations). The synthetic corrosion solution was used for optimization.

The comparative performance of the conventional concentric nebulizer operating at a sample uptake rate of 0.8 ml min^{-1} and two low-flow Micromist nebulizers with sample uptake rates of 100 µl min^{-1} and 50 µl min^{-1} revealed that the optima of the nebulizer flow rate were 0.92 ml min^{-1}, 0.97 ml min^{-1} and 1.06 ml min^{-1} for conventional and Micromist nebulizers, respectively (Table 10).

Table 10. Analytical performance of Micromist nebulizers in comparison to conventional concentric nebulizer.

Nebulizer	Conventional concentric	MMN100	MMN50
Sample uptake rate, µl min^{-1}	800	100	50
Nebulizer flow rate, ml min^{-1}	0.92	0.97	1.06
CeO^{+}/Ce^{+} ratio	0.010	0.012	0.011
Ba^{++}/Ba^{+} ratio	0.010	0.007	0.007
Al intensity (20µg L^{-1})	1123387	729637	566933
Mg intensity (10 µg L^{-1})	147175	98256	77780
Rh intensity (10 µg L^{-1})	277361	165532	133496

The maximum signal intensity was shifted to the higher values of the nebulizer flow rate for the Micromist nebulizers, which can be probably attributed to the change in aerosol characteristics [86]. Fig. 3.2 shows the Al, Mg and Rh signal intensities, as well as Ba^{++}/Ba^+ and CeO^+/Ce^+ ratios as functions of the nebulizer gas flow rate for Micromist nebulizer (50 µl min^{-1}).

The peak maxima positions were identical and no variation of the nebulizer flow rate optimum for Al, Mg and Rh signals were observed. Thus, the optimum value of the nebulizer gas flow can easily be chosen without any intensity loss for different signals monitored. The results of the optimized performance of MMN 50 and MMN 100 as compared to the conventional concentric nebulizer are summarized in Table 10.

Even with high salt matrix, both low-flow nebulizers showed a precision of 2-3 % RSDs and Ba^{++}/Ba^+ and CeO^+/Ce^+ ratios below 2% levels at the optimum nebulizer gas flow rate (Fig. 3.2). A long-term stability test with the above mentioned synthetic corrosion solution revealed that both Micromist low-flow nebulizers are suitable for long-term operation with low risk of nebulizer tip-clogging.

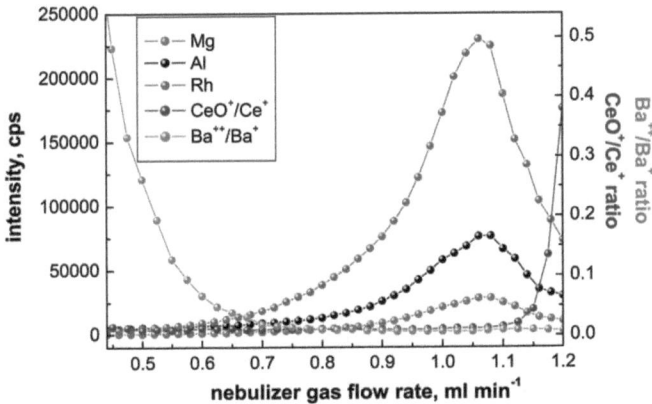

Fig. 3.2. Al, Mg and Rh signal intensity profiles as a function of nebulizer gas flow rate for Micromist nebulizer with an uptake rate 50 µl min^{-1} as well as the influence of the nebulizer gas flow rate on Ba^{++}/Ba^+ and CeO^+/Ce^+ ratios.

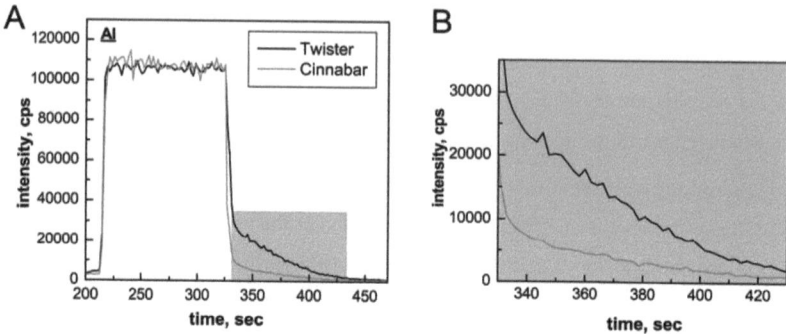

Fig. 3.3. Wash-out profile of Al signal in a synthetic corrosion solution for a conventional cyclonic spray chamber (Twister, 40 cm^3) and a mini-cyclonic spray chamber with the reduced inner volume (Cinnabar, 20 cm^3).

A fast wash-out is a critical parameter in element-specific and time-resolved corrosion research, especially since high sample throughput is needed. Online, time-dependent transient introduction of corrosion probes into ICP-MS requires keeping the wash-out times as short as possible. Thus, the performance of a Cinnabar spray chamber (20 cm^3 internal volume) in combination with Micromist, operating at 50 µl min^{-1}, was studied in terms of wash-out times for solutions with high salt matrix. Fig. 3.3 shows the wash-out profiles of Al signal for the mentioned synthetic corrosion solution. According to Todoli *et al.* [80] the wash-out time is defined as the time required for a signal drop down to 1% of its steady value. As it can be concluded from Fig. 3.3B, the Cinnabar spray chamber provides significantly shorter wash-out times of only 90 s, whereas a wash-out time of 130 s was determined for the conventional cyclonic spray chamber.

Thus, the alternative introduction system, consisting of the low-flow nebulizer Micromist and Cinnabar spray chamber proved to show stable and efficient performance as coupled online to microcapillary set-up via FIAS. Online monitoring of the element release during corrosion experiments is possible with the optimized alternative ICP-MS introduction system, operating at low sample uptake rates and providing short wash-out times of the corrosion probes.

3.3.2. Matrix effects.

Various inorganic salts and acids in a wide range of concentrations, *e.g.* NaCl, Na_2SO_4, HCl, HNO_3 or H_2SO_4, are typical media in corrosion experiments. In continuous flow a dilution would be needed to deal with a high TDS content of the corrosion probes and to minimize the matrix load on the ICP-MS instrument. However, for local corrosion investigations a dilution is not desirable, because only low dissolution rates of the secondary alloying elements (*e.g.* Cu, Mn) can be predicted during corrosion initiation. Thus, important information about element-specific dissolution rates of secondary elements would be lost in case of the dilution. Hence, a transient online introduction of the undiluted corrosion probes to ICP-MS *via* FIAS was suggested to minimize matrix load.

The degree of sodium chloride matrix effects was assessed in the continuous *vs.* flow injection mode. The degree of signal suppression in the synthetic corrosive solution, which contains 0.1 M NaCl as a matrix, in the case of the continuous nebulization was on average 5-15% as compared to the same synthetic corrosion solution in 1% HNO_3 (Table 11). The degree of the signal suppression was non-uniform across the mass range. The signals obtained in sodium chloride solution were also characterized by slightly higher RSDs, *i.e.* 0.1-1% for non-matrix and 1-5% for matrix solutions. The flow injection introduction of the samples with NaCl caused lower matrix suppression, typically only 4-7%.

Table 11. Signal suppression of intensities caused by 0.1 M NaCl solution as a matrix.

Analyte ion	Non-matrix solution		Matrix solution		Suppression, %
	Intensity, cps	RSD, %	Intensity, cps	RSD, %	
$^{24}Mg^+$	38330	0.72	34852	1.76	9.1
$^{27}Al^+$	118499	0.84	103846	1.84	12.4
$^{52}Cr^+$	16220	0.13	16448	1.91	-1.4
$^{55}Mn^+$	21618	0.12	20612	1.62	4.7
$^{57}Fe^+$	4768	0.66	4127	1.09	13.4

⁶⁵Cu⁺	3934	1.06	3623	5.54	7.9
¹⁰³Rh⁺	262567	0.41	225621	1.41	14.1

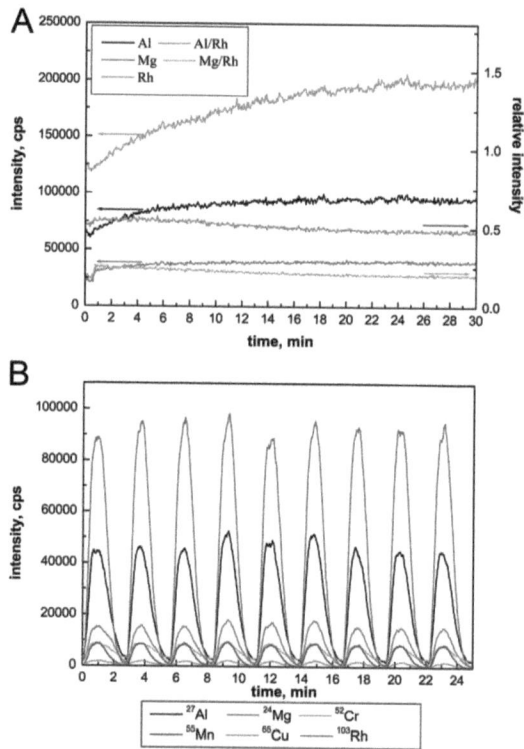

Fig. 3.4. Influence of 0.1 M NaCl matrix on long-term stability of signal intensities: A. continuous ICP-MS vs. B. FI-ICP-MS.

Fig. 3.4 shows an impact of 0.1 M NaCl matrix on the long-term signal stability of Al, Mg and Rh in the case of continuous nebulization vs. the transient peak profiles in the FI mode for the same elements. Fig. 3.4A reveals that the continuous introduction of high NaCl concentration caused a long-term drift of the signal. Even with the low-flow Micromist nebulizer, operating at a sample uptake rate of 50 µl min⁻¹, an average time of 10-20 min was required for signal stabilization. The comparison of Fig. 3.4A and Fig. 3.4B clearly demonstrates the advantage of a transient sample introduction using FI mode. The peak profiles obtained in FI-ICP-MS are characterized by much better long-term stability for all signals monitored. Generally, the matrix suppression is less profound in FI-ICP-MS, since only small quantities of the corrosion solution are introduced into ICP-MS. Moreover, dispersion processes, which occur in the flow manifold, also reduce the matrix load on the instrument.

Different strategies can be applied to overcome the matrix influence on the signal intensities: internal standardization, standard addition method or a calibration with matrix matched standards solutions. In ICP-MS the use of an internal standard is most common. However, the addition of an internal standard to the corrosive medium circulating in the microflow-capillary was difficult to implement, since on one hand internal standards are usually prepared in acid solutions. This lowers the pH of the medium, which has a huge influence on the corrosion process and the dissolution behaviour. On the other hand, an additional standard could precipitate on the surface of the alloy during the corrosion process [135].

A later addition of the internal standard *via* chemifold is less precise and could not be managed with the here presented FIAS set-up. Procedures like standard addition calibrations are relatively time consuming and are not suitable for online multi-element local corrosion analysis. Hence, a matrix matched calibration strategy was evaluated and later on used in all further corrosion experiments to compensate NaCl matrix influence.

3.3.3. Optimization of the flow injection system.

To improve the performance of the FIAS with respect to the analysis of the corrosion probes, various flow injection parameters (*e.g.* sample uptake rate) as well as different calibration strategies and LODs for FI-ICP-MS were assessed and optimized. Fig. 3.5 shows an influence of the sample uptake rate on the peak shape profile exemplary for Al in the corrosion solution. As expected, an increase of the sample uptake rate from 60 µl min^{-1} to 200 µl min^{-1} caused an increase in peak height. Relatively low sample uptake rates of 60-80 µl min^{-1} induced the broadening of the peaks and increase of the peak acquirement time. Fig. 3.6A demonstrates the influence of the sample uptake rate on the peak area *vs.* the peak height intensity. The influence of the same parameter on the relative standard deviation is shown in Fig. 3.6B. Both Fig. 3.6A and Fig. 3.6B clearly point out that the optimum of the sample uptake rate should be chosen to provide the best precision of the measurements.

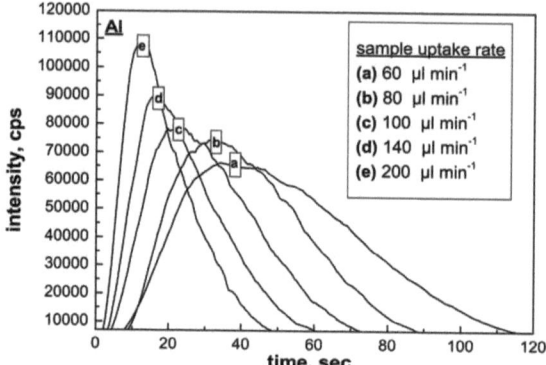

Fig. 3.5. Al peak profiles in the synthetic corrosion solution as a function of sample uptake rate.

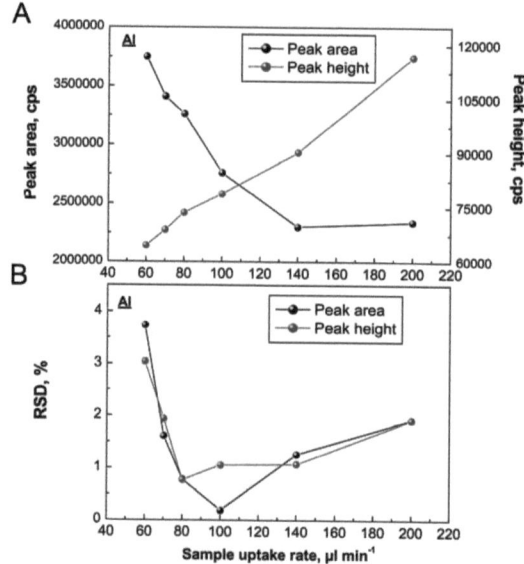

Fig. 3.6. Influence of the sample uptake rate on A. peak height *vs.* peak area signal; B. precision of the measurements.

The sample uptake rate has an opposite effect on peak area and peak height signals, whereas the RSD curve goes through a minimum at the 100 µl min^{-1}. Thus, a sample uptake rate of 100 µl min^{-1} was finally chosen for all later corrosion tests.

Due to the fact, that the total volume used in the capillary set-up was limited by 250 µl, the sample loop volume was finally set to 20 µl. The low volume of the sample loop minimizes the load of high matrix concentration (0.1 M NaCl) on the instrument. Moreover, the small loop volume prevents the excessive dilution of circulating corrosive medium, when a new portion of fresh 0.1 M NaCl solution is introduced into the capillary flow. Beside FIAS optimization, different calibration strategies based on peak height and peak area measurements for non-matrix matched and matrix matched calibrations were assessed.

Table 12. Comparison of the calibration procedures in FI-ICP-MS mode performed with and without 0.1 M NaCl matrix matching to the continuous nebulization mode with internal standardization (Rh as internal standard).

Analyte ion	Non-matrix matched calibration FIAS				Matrix matched calibration FIAS				Continuous nebulization with internal standardization	
	Height		Area		Height		Area			
	µg L^{-1}	RSD, %	µg L^{-1}	RSD, %	µg L^{-1}	RSD, %	µg L^{-1}	RSD, %	µg L^{-1}	RSD, %
$^{24}Mg^+$	8.7	1.34	7.7	2.24	10.7	2.32	9.1	3.57	10.3	0.72
$^{27}Al^+$	17.6	1.05	17.8	0.19	21.1	2.08	20.1	1.95	21.4	0.84
$^{52}Cr^+$	1.8	2.36	1.4	5.21	2.2	0.58	1.5	2.92	1.4	0.13
$^{55}Mn^+$	1.1	2.63	1.1	1.73	1.4	1.00	1.2	0.86	1.2	0.12
$^{65}Cu^+$	1.6	1.40	1.3	6.85	2.2	2.34	1.6	4.25	1.3	1.06

Table 12 presents the comparison of the different calibration procedures. Results calculated based on non-matrix matched calibration were characterized by an average recovery of ~80-90% in comparison to measurements in continuous mode with internal standardization. Results achieved with matrix matched calibration in FIAS mode derived a much better agreement with the results in continuous nebulization mode (~95-99% recovery).

Therefore, it can be concluded, that for all selected elements the use of matrix-matched calibration is advantageous over the non-matrix matched calibration procedure. A comparison of the concentrations calculated for peak area and for peak height showed that peak height gives better recoveries for main alloying elements (Al, Mg), whereas peak area data were characterized by slightly better precision and recoveries for secondary alloying elements. The correlation coefficients R^2 obtained for the peak height calibration were generally better than for peak area calibration, e.g. $R^2_{Al}= 0.9998$ and $R^2_{Mg} = 0.9997$ vs. $R^2_{Al}= 0.9992$ and $R^2_{Mg} = 0.9981$ for peak height and peak area, respectively. Thus, peak height data were used for all signals monitored and peak area data were additionally monitored for Cu and Mn.

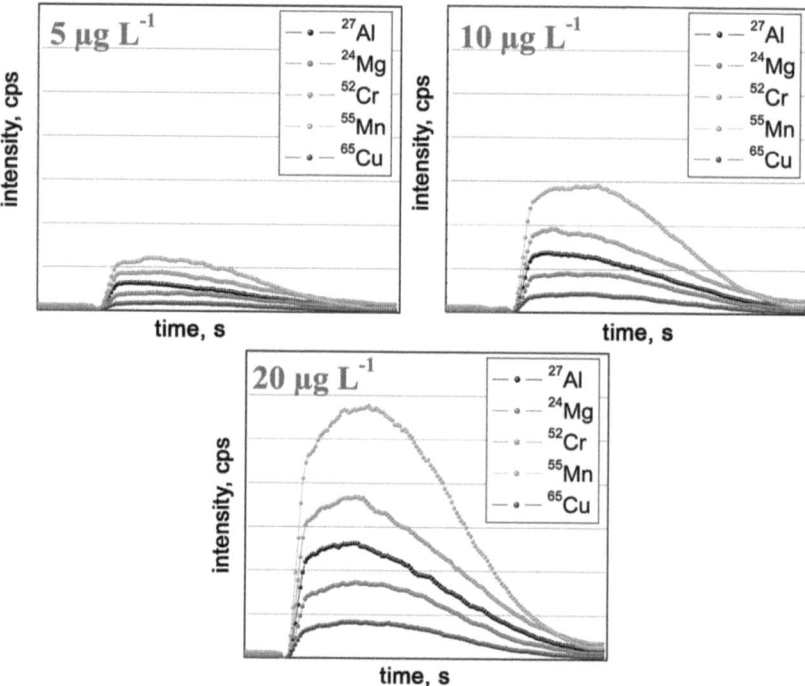

Fig. 3.7. Exemplary multi-element calibration profiles for a synthetic corrosion solution with the concentrations of 5 µg L⁻¹, 10 µg L⁻¹ and 20 µg L⁻¹, containing 0.1 M NaCl as a matrix.

Limits of detection for the analytes monitored in the FI mode were calculated as three times of the standard deviation (σ) of the analytes peak height of 5 blank solutions. The FI-ICP-MS LODs in µg L⁻¹ and equivalent LODs in µg cm⁻² are summarized in Table 13 in comparison to the LODs for the continuous nebulization ICP-MS mode. For the blank solutions, FI-ICP-MS gave about 2-10 times higher LODs, than continuous ICP-MS (instrumental LODs). However, when LODs are calculated for the complete finial application, FI-ICP-MS provides better detection limits than continuous ICP-MS, because a 20- to 40-fold dilution of the corrosion probes is required for analysis in continuous ICP-MS mode. This dilution factor needs to be taken into account for the calculation of the method related detection limits (MDLs).

Fig. 3.7. depicts exemplary multi-element calibration profiles with 0.1 M NaCl as a matrix. Final matrix matched calibration curves for Al, Mg, Cr, Cu and Mn together with the correlation coefficients are presented in Fig. 3.8.

Table 13. ICP-MS and FI-ICP-MS detection limits for elements monitored, in $\mu g\ L^{-1}$ and equivalent $\mu g\ cm^{-2}$ units (MDLs are calculated taking a 20-fold dilution into account).

Analyte	Detection limits, $\mu g\ L^{-1}$			Equivalent detection limits, $\mu g\ cm^{-2}$		
	LOD ICP-MS	MDL ICP-MS	LOD = MDL FI-ICP-MS	LOD ICP-MS	MDL ICP-MS	LOD = MDL FI-ICP-MS
$^{24}Mg^+$	0.02	0.4	0.22	0.002	0.04	0.02
$^{27}Al^+$	0.03	0.6	0.19	0.003	0.06	0.02
$^{55}Mn^+$	0.02	0.4	0.03	0.002	0.04	0.002
$^{65}Cu^+$	0.01	0.1	0.12	0.001	0.01	0.01

3.3.4. Online time- and element-resolved corrosion investigation of AA 6111.

After careful optimization of the microflow-capillary FI-ICP-MS set-up the efficiency of the technique was proved by a multi-element monitoring of the corrosion dependent release of primary and secondary alloying elements from a commercial available Al alloy AA 6111.

Alloy microstructure.

Al alloy AA 6111, typically used in aerospace and automotive industries, is characterized by the presence of several types of intermetallic phases (Fig. 3.9). The predominant intermetallic phases present in AA 6111 are Mg_2Si (visible in the optical microscope image in black colour), Al(Fe, Mn, Si) (in light grey colour) and Q-phase

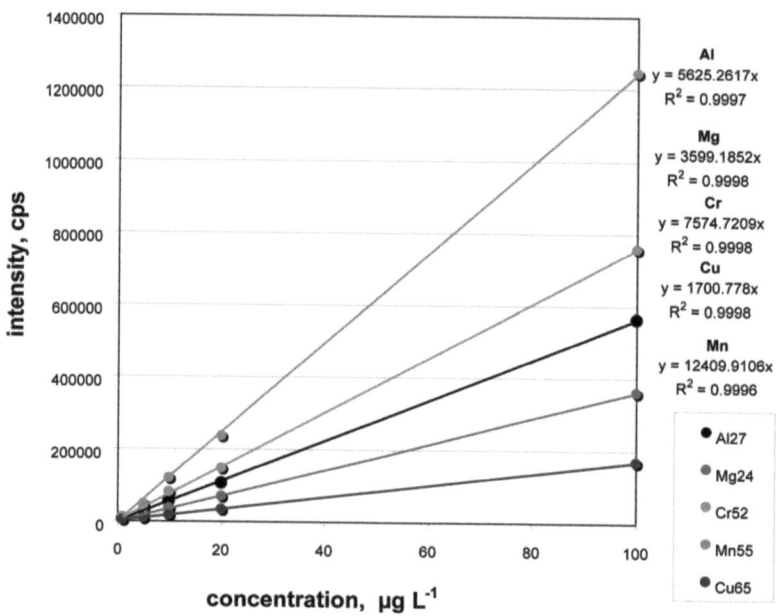

Fig. 3.8. Matrix matched calibration curves for Al, Mg, Cr, Cu and Mn.

Al(Cu, Mg, Si) [136, 137]. The Mg_2Si phase is described by a corrosion potential lower than the matrix and behaves as anodic site. Hence, dissolution of these inclusions during pitting corrosion is expected. Al(Fe, Mn, Si) particles act as cathodes during the corrosion attack and promote dissolution of the matrix. Al(Cu, Mg, Si) phase has a corrosion potential close to the alloy matrix.

In the present study the simultaneous time-resolved release of four elements Al, Mg, Cu and Mn from AA 6111 was studied with signal acquisition every 6 minutes during the first two hours of the corrosion process. Generally, the maximum sampling frequency of the FI-ICP-MS set-up depends both on the FI program parameters, ICP-MS measurement parameters (readings per replicate, dwell time, number of elements, etc.) and the dissolution process itself. For typical Al alloys the sampling frequency can be as fast as every 1-2 min, when highly corrosive media are used.

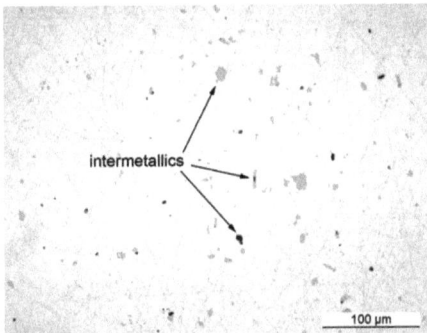

Fig. 3.9. Optical microscope image of AA 6111, revealing its microstructure.

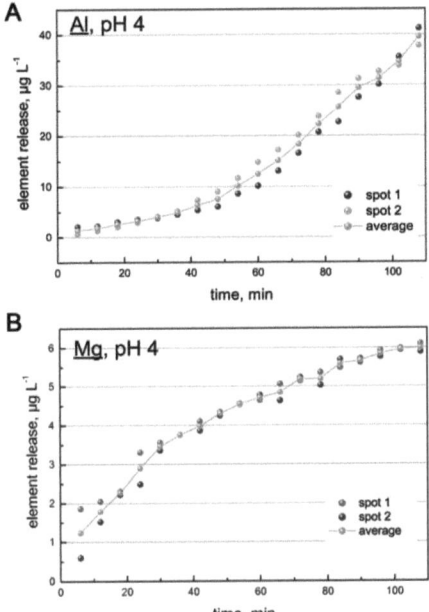

Fig. 3.10. Measurements of Al and Mg release preformed at two random spots of the alloy (0.1 M NaCl, pH 4.0).

To confirm the representativeness of the FI-ICP-MS results, the corrosion tests with NaCl medium (pH 4.0) were performed on two random spots of the alloy specimen. The results are described by

RSDs < 15% (Fig. 3.10). Whereas, this difference in the results is most probably explained by the local microstructure difference of these two sample spots, the FI-ICP-MS technique itself provides representative data.

Dissolution of Al.

Fig. 3.11A shows the results of *in situ* online monitoring of Al dissolution from AA 6111 as a function of the exposure time and pH value of the corrosive medium. The measured concentrations of Al dissolving from AA 6111 in $\mu g\ L^{-1}$ were converted to $\mu g\ cm^{-2}$.

A clear influence of the pH value of NaCl solution on the dissolution rate of Al is demonstrated in Fig. 3.11A. The more acidic the corrosive medium the higher dissolution rate of Al is observed. The results are in good agreement with the stability of the oxide film layer, which is naturally formed on the alloy surface, at different pH values. For Al alloys, the layer of the oxide is usually stable in the range of pH 4-10. The stability of the oxide layer down to a pH of 4.0 is also the reason, why only a slightly higher Al release was observed at pH 4.0 in comparison to pH 6.0, whereas at pH 2.0 a much higher release of Al was revealed. Hence, the acidic medium at pH 2.0 promotes a much faster dissolution of the protective oxide layer, leading consequently to the faster dissolution of Al.

It can be also observed from Fig. 3.11A that the curve of the Al release at pH 2.0 changes its slope after about 40-60 min of the corrosion process. The acceleration of dissolution rate after this time can be most probably attributed to the fact that a certain initiation time is required to break down the protective oxide film before a significant release of the Al from the matrix starts.

Generally, both oxide layer stability and the microstructure heterogeneity have an impact on the Al release tendency. Intermetallic particles of Al(Fe, Mn, Si) type serve as local cathode sites of the pitting corrosion, causing the anodic dissolution of the Al matrix around them.

Dissolution of Mg.

The dissolution behaviour of Mg from AA 6111 in NaCl medium is presented in Fig. 3.11B. It can be concluded from the data that the release of Mg in neutral medium (pH 4.0 and pH 6.0) differs significantly from the dissolution behaviour in acidic medium (pH 2.0). The release of Mg in Al alloys is mainly caused by the anodic nature of Mg_2Si particles and is in agreement with studies from other authors [15, 43]. Mg dissolution from inclusions is a relatively fast process, which explains the pronounced primary dissolution curve behaviour. After all Mg from Mg_2Si

intermetallic particles is dissolved, the dissolution curve reaches a quasi-plateau state (Fig. 3.11B). The plateaus are reached after about 45 min at pH 4 and after about 60 min at pH 6.

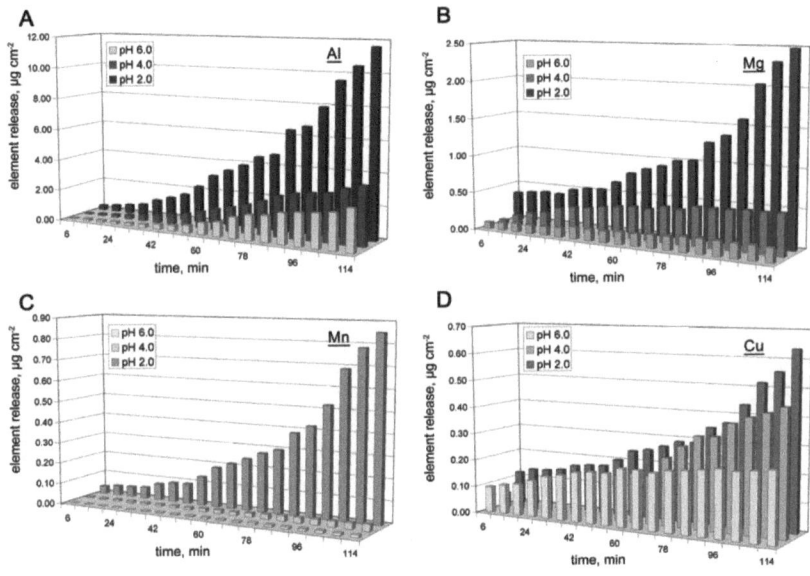

Fig. 3.11. Time-resolved dissolution behaviour of A. Al; B. Mg; C. Mn and D. Cu in 0.1 M NaCl corrosive medium at three different pH values.

The difference of the dissolution behaviour in acidic medium can be explained by the higher dissolution rate of Mg at low pH values. At neutral pH Mg forms corrosion products during the dissolution process, *e.g.* magnesium hydroxide, which precipitates on the alloy surface, thus lowering the slope of the dissolution curve. In the acidic medium the process of the precipitation is assumed to be hindered.

Thus, it was demonstrated that novel FI-ICP-MS set-up enables in situ quantitative monitoring of dissolution processes of the main alloying elements from matrix and inclusions with a high time resolution. This was shown for Al and Mg release from AA 6111 aluminium alloy. The proposed technique is remarkably distinguished by a high throughput of the analysis compared to the standard element-specific methods used in corrosion research (*e.g.* SEM-EDX usually requires a time-consumable sample preparation step for quantification of dissolution processes from the alloy).

Dissolution of Mn and Cu.

A further advantage of the novel *in situ* FI-ICP-MS set-up is the possibility to monitor also the release of low concentrated secondary alloying elements, *e.g.* Mn and Cu. Fig. 3.11C and Fig. 3.11D present the dissolution behaviour of Mn and Cu from AA 6111 at different pH values. The tendency of Mn to dissolve in acidic NaCl solution is completely different from the dissolution at neutral pH. As mentioned above, Mn is mainly present in Al(Fe, Mn, Si) intermetallic particles, which behave as local cathodes in the corrosion process. Generally, at neutral pH these particles do not dissolve, but promote the dissolution of Al matrix around the inclusions. This fact most probably explains the observed very low dissolution rate of Mn at pH 4.0 and pH 6.0 (Fig. 3.11C). A much higher dissolution rate of Mn is revealed at pH 2.0. The release of Mn in acidic medium is attributed to uniform corrosion process, which is not related to the electrochemical nature of Al(Fe, Mn, Si) phase.

Fig. 3.11D represents the release of Cu from AA 6111. For Cu the same tendency of an increasing dissolution rate with the decrease of pH can be observed. Generally, the exact behaviour of Cu dissolution is more difficult to predict, due to the fact that Cu is present in the alloy not only in the Q-phase, but it can also be spread in Cu-depleted zones along grain boundaries, which are described as anodic relative to the matrix and therefore tend to dissolve [42]. However, a notable increase of Cu dissolution rate in the acidic medium can also be attributed to the uniform corrosion process.

It can be summarized that the investigation of pH influence on the corrosion processes revealed that the specific dissolution behaviour in NaCl solution strongly depends on specific properties and origins (matrix or inclusion) for each element. Moreover, the element-specific investigation of corrosion behaviour of AA 6111 revealed a relatively high release of the secondary alloying element Cu in studied range of pHs. This brings new information on the behaviour of Cu during the corrosion process, which is so far not fully understood.

3.4. Conclusions.

It was demonstrated that the online microflow-capillary FI-ICP-MS set-up described in this Chapter enables *in situ* element- and time-resolved investigations of localized corrosion processes. Not only the dissolutions of main alloying elements are accessible, but also the release behaviour of secondary alloying elements can be monitored during time-resolved corrosion investigations. The optimization of the microflow sample introduction system and the flow injection characteristics resulted in a precise and reliable signal acquisition in FI analysis mode and gave comparable results to conventional ICP-MS analysis of diluted samples with internal standardization.

The transient sample introduction *via* FIAS allows the introduction of small aliquots for analysis, which enables a time-resolved monitoring of corrosion experiments. Moreover, the transient sample introduction minimized the signal drift due to high salt load on the ICP-MS instrument, especially when high salt matrices such as 0.1 M sodium chloride solution were used as corrosive medium.

The efficiency of the new online hyphenation of the microcapillary set-up to ICP-MS *via* a flow injection manifold was clearly demonstrated by investigation of the dissolution rates of main (Al, Mg) and secondary (Mn, Cu) alloying elements from the aluminium alloy AA 6111.

4. Element-specific *in situ* corrosion behaviour of Zr-Cu-Ni-Al-Nb bulk metallic glass in acidic media studied using online microflow-capillary FI-ICP-MS technique.

(partly published in: N. Homazava, A. Shkabko, D. Logvinovich, U. Krähenbühl, A. Ulrich, Element-specific in situ corrosion behaviour of Zr-Cu-Ni-Al-Nb bulk metallic glass in acidic media studied using a novel microcapillary flow injection inductively coupled plasma mass spectrometry technique, Intermetallics 16 (2008) 1066-1072 [138].)

4.1. Overview.

This Chapter presents the applicability of the microflow-capillary FI-ICP-MS technique for the element-specific time-resolved *in situ* corrosion susceptibility study of the $Zr_{58.5}Cu_{15.6}Ni_{12.8}Al_{10.3}Nb_{2.8}$ bulk metallic glass.

Zr-based bulk metallic glasses are a recent class of amorphous materials with excellent mechanical properties (*e.g.* low Young's modulus, high specific strength) and good chemical resistance [116, 139], which are especially prominent for several industrial needs as well as medical applications. Fig. 4.1 shows a progress in the fabrication of new bulk metallic glass over the past 40 years.

Recently, a completely new application area of Zr-BMGs has been discovered. Zr-BMG with a composition of $Zr_{58.5}Cu_{15.6}Ni_{12.8}Al_{10.3}Nb_{2.8}$ (Vitreloy 106a), which was developed at California Institute of Technology [140], was used as a collector for solar noble gases on NASA's Genesis mission [141, 142]. This information is essential for the evaluation of the energy distribution of solar particles. To provoke a later noble gases release and to access gases depth distribution data a novel technique of Zr-BMG step-wise acidic etching was used to ensure a homogeneous release of the sampled gases. Therefore, the information on time- and element-resolved nature of Zr-BMG corrosion dissolution behaviour is especially significant to estimate its relevant characteristics, *e.g.* preferential element release during the etching procedure, when Zr-BMG is used as a solar wind collector. Since Zr-BMGs are also interesting new materials for medical applications, the corrosion behaviour needs to be investigated with respect to metal ions release for biocompatibility [73, 143] and cytotoxicity applications [144].

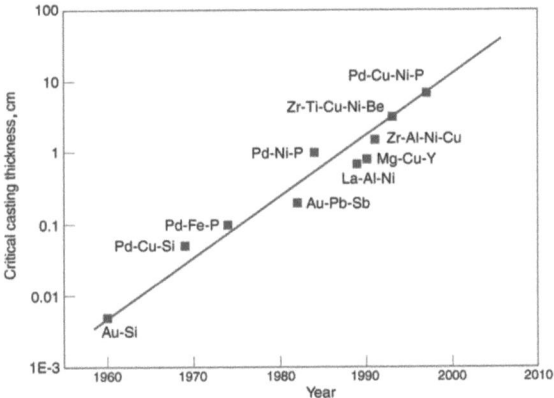

Fig. 4.1. Progress in the synthesis of the bulk metallic glasses over the past 40 years [118].

Zander and Köster [145] reviewed different corrosion investigations of amorphous and nano-crystalline Zr-BMGs in various corrosive media. Hiromoto *et. al* [50, 51] studied the effects of the surface finishing, chloride ion concentration, dissolved oxygen content on the polarization effect for $Zr_{65}Al_{7.5}Ni_{10}Cu_{17.5}$. Electrochemical investigations of the Zr-BMG with the same composition were also performed in 0.1 M Na_2SO_4 solutions within pH range from 2 to 8 [45]. The corrosion behaviour of the same bulk metallic glass type was studied in acidic solutions by Dhawan *et. al* [146] using potentiodynamic polarization measurements. Recently it was also experimentally proven that the addition of Nb can significantly improve the corrosion resistance of Zr-bulk metallic glasses [48, 49, 52, 139, 147].

However, so far the majority of the corrosion studies on Zr-BMG were performed using electrochemical polarization or weight loss measurements. Only two recent papers presented element-resolved release data of Zr-Cu-Ni-Al-Nb BMG after static immersion test [49, 73]. However, information on time-resolved element-specific dissolution behaviour of Zr-BMG could not be found in the literature.

The aim of the present Chapter is to investigate *in situ* element-specific and time-resolved corrosion susceptibility characteristics of $Zr_{58.5}Cu_{15.6}Ni_{12.8}Al_{10.3}Nb_{2.8}$ in two different acidic media 1M HCl and 1M HNO_3 using the new microcapillary FI-ICP-MS technique. The investigation of the corrosion behaviour of Zr-BMGs in these acidic solutions can provide novel and valuable information, when the Zr-BMG material is used for noble gases collection and later on leached to provoke the gas release. To support the investigation of the corrosion processes, X-ray photoelectron spectroscopy (XPS) analysis of the Zr-BMG surface was performed before and after immersion in 1M HCl. The data were compared to the results from the microcapillary FI-ICP-MS measurements.

4.2. Experimental.

4.2.1. Microflow-capillary FI-ICP-MS set-up.

The design of the microflow-capillary FI-ICP-MS set-up used in this Chapter is the same as the one presented in Chapter 3. The microcapillary, containing the corrosive medium, was positioned on a Zr-BMG surface. A capillary with an internal diameter of 0.8 mm was used for all tests. The total volume of corrosive medium used within the capillary was 320 µl. The medium was pumped within the capillary with a cycling flux of 500 µl min^{-1}. A computer controlled flow injection analysis system FIAS-200 (Perkin Elmer/Sciex) was used for online *in situ* introduction of corrosion medium probes into an ICP-MS in time intervals of 10 minutes over 3 hours.

The volume of a single corrosion aliquot was determined by the volume of the FI sample loop (20 µl). The removed aliquots were replaced by fresh solution of the corrosive medium. Dilution factors were taken into account for data evaluation. The multi-element specific analysis of corrosion probes was performed using a quadrupole ICP-MS instrument ELAN 6000 (Perkin Elmer/Sciex).

Table 14. ICP-MS operating conditions

ICP-MS Instrument	ELAN 6000
Plasma parameters	
RF Power (W)	1100
Coolant gas flow-rate (L min^{-1})	15
Auxiliary gas flow-rate (L min^{-1})	1

Nebulizer gas flow-rate (L min^{-1})	0.98
Ion-sampling parameters	
Sampling and skimmer cones	Nickel
Data acquisition parameters	
Dwell time (ms)	30
Readings per replicate	400
Number of replicates	17
Analytes monitored	^{27}Al$^+$, ^{60}Ni$^+$, ^{63}Cu$^+$, ^{90}Zr$^+$, ^{93}Nb$^+$

The sample introduction system of the instrument consisted of a low flow Micromist nebulizer (Glass Expansion, Australia), which operated at the sample uptake rate of 100 µl min^{-1}, and a Cinnabar spray chamber with an inner volume of 20 cm^3. The operating conditions and details of the ICP-MS analysis are described in Table 14.

4.2.2. X-ray diffraction and X-ray photoelectron spectroscopy.

The long-range structure of $Zr_{58.5}Cu_{15.6}Ni_{12.8}Al_{10.3}Nb_{2.8}$ was checked by X-ray diffraction using a Phillips X'Pert PRO MPD Θ-Θ System (Cu Kα radiation) equipped with a linear detector (X'Celerator). X-ray data were collected in both Θ-Θ and grazing incidence modes (at grazing angles of 0.05-1°) in the angular range of 10-80° with a step size of 0.017° and counting time of 200 seconds per data point.

Additionally, investigation of the oxide film of $Zr_{58.5}Cu_{15.6}Ni_{12.8}Al_{10.3}Nb_{2.8}$ before and after immersion in acid (1 M HCl for 16 hours) was performed by X-ray photoelectron spectroscopy. The XPS spectra of Zr 3d, Nb 3d, Al 2s, Cu 2p, Ni 2p and O 1s were acquired on a PHI Quantum 2000 spectrometer with monochromatic Al Kα radiation (1486.6 eV). The hemispherical energy analyzer was operated with constant pass energy of 58.7 eV for high resolution spectra. The spectra were collected at room temperature at a photoelectron take off angle of 45° with respect to the surface plane. The sample charging was neutralized with electron flood and ion guns. All the spectra were referenced to the C 1s line (285 eV) and Au 4f$_{7/2}$ line (84 eV). The XPS spectra were background subtracted using the Shirley method. The intensity ratios were evaluated using sensitivity factors supplied by the instrument manufacturer.

4.2.3. Materials and chemicals.

Element-specific corrosion dissolution behaviour of Zr-bulk metallic glass with a composition of $Zr_{58.5}Cu_{15.6}Ni_{12.8}Al_{10.3}Nb_{2.8}$ (at. %) was investigated in 1M HCl and 1M HNO_3. The sample with a size of 20 mm × 10 mm was prepared according to [140]. The surface of the sample was polished with a diamond paste down to 0.25 µm (mirror-like quality). Then, the sample was cleaned with ethanol in an ultrasonic bath, dried at ambient air and further exposed to air for at least 24 h to ensure a proper formation of an oxide film.

One molar hydrochloric acid (1 M HCl) and one molar nitric acid (1 M HNO_3) solutions were prepared from concentrated HCl and HNO_3 of ultrapur quality (Merck, Germany). Single element stock solutions of ICP-MS quality (1000 mg L^{-1}, Merck, Germany) were step-wise diluted to prepare standard solutions, containing 0.01, 0.1 and 1 µg L^{-1} of Zr, Nb, Al, Cu and Ni in 1 M HCl and 1M HNO_3, respectively. These solutions were used for the ICP-MS calibration procedure. Results were calculated based on peak maximum of the transient FI-ICP-MS signals. All solutions were prepared using 18.2 MΩ cm ultrapure water (Milli-Q Gradient A10 supply system, Millipore, MA, USA).

4.3. Results and discussion.

Fig. 4.2 shows the X-ray diffraction pattern of $Zr_{58.5}Cu_{15.6}Ni_{12.8}Al_{10.3}Nb_{2.8}$. The broad characteristic diffraction reflection at 2Θ of about 39° is clearly observed. No sharp peaks corresponding to the crystalline phases were identified. Moreover, the measurement at grazing angle as low as 0.05° also did not reveal the presence of any crystalline phases in the material. An additional examination of the sample polished surface in secondary electron microscope confirmed the absence of any secondary phases. Thus, $Zr_{58.5}Cu_{15.6}Ni_{12.8}Al_{10.3}Nb_{2.8}$ was proven to be fully amorphous.

The detection limits of all elements potentially dissolved from $Zr_{58.5}Cu_{15.6}Ni_{12.8}Al_{10.3}Nb_{2.8}$ were calculated based on a three Sigma method (3σ-method). Limits of detection for ^{27}Al, ^{60}Ni, ^{63}Cu, ^{90}Zr and ^{93}Nb are derived as three times of the standard deviation (σ) of the average element signal measured in the blank solutions ($n = 5$).

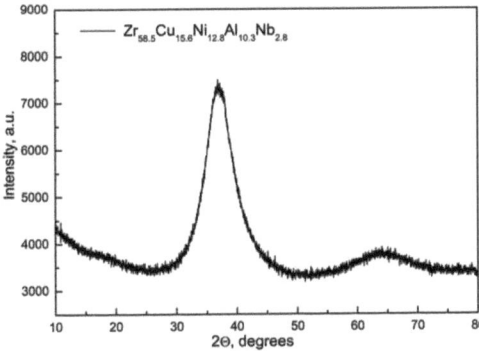

Fig. 4.2. X-ray diffraction pattern of $Zr_{58.5}Cu_{15.6}Ni_{12.8}Al_{10.3}Nb_{2.8}$.

Table 15 summarizes the LODs calculated for the solutions in ng L^{-1} and equivalent LODs for the exposed area in ng cm^{-2} determined according to the equation:

$$LOD_{ng \cdot cm^{-2}} = LOD_{ng \cdot L^{-1}} \cdot \frac{V}{S}, \text{ where} \qquad (4.1)$$

V is the volume of the corrosive liquid in the microflow-capillary;

S is the area of the sample surface exposed to the corrosion attack.

Table 15. Microcapillary FI-ICP-MS limits of detection for elements analyzed, in ng L^{-1} and ng cm^{-2}.

Analyte	Detection limits in the solution, ng L^{-1}	Equivalent detection limits based on the exposed area, ng cm^{-2}
$^{90}Zr^+$	3	0.19
$^{93}Nb^+$	2	0.13
$^{27}Al^+$	280	17.8
$^{63}Cu^+$	30	1.9
$^{60}Ni^+$	40	2.6

Thus, according to the equation, the volume of the corrosive liquid medium (*V*) should be kept at minimum to provide low limits of detection. In the present study, the total volume of the corrosive liquid was minimized to 320 μl, whereas the aliquots analyzed in time intervals of 10 minutes were 20 μl only. The achieved low LODs at the level of 1-20 ng cm^{-2} granted the possibility to investigate the corrosion behaviour of $Zr_{58.5}Cu_{15.6}Ni_{12.8}Al_{10.3}Nb_{2.8}$ already at the initial stages of the corrosion attack.

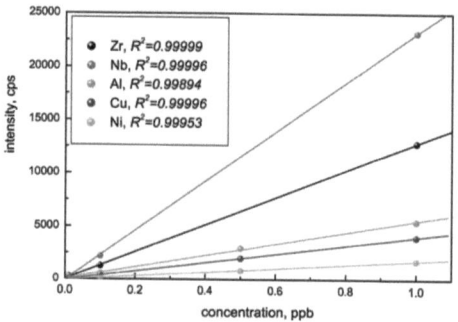

Fig. 4.3. Matrix matched calibration curves for Zr, Nb, Al, Cu and Ni.

Matrix matched calibration curves for Zr, Nb, Al, Cu and Ni together with the correlation coefficients are shown in Fig. 4.3.

Fig. 4.4 demonstrates time-resolved profiles of the measured element releases for Zr, Nb (A) and Al, Cu, Ni (B) from $Zr_{58.5}Cu_{15.6}Ni_{12.8}Al_{10.3}Nb_{2.8}$ exposed to 1 M HCl under open circuit potential conditions. All measurements were performed as triple determinations. Triple determinations mean that every *in situ* measurement was repeated at three random spots of the bulk metallic glass. Error bars are related to the standard deviation of these triple determinations.

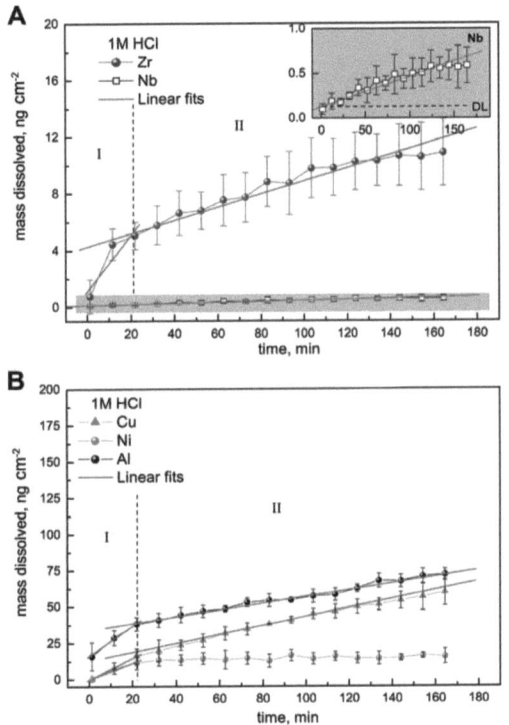

Fig. 4.4. Time-resolved dissolution rates of $Zr_{58.5}Cu_{15.6}Ni_{12.8}Al_{10.3}Nb_{2.8}$ constituent elements: A. Zr, Nb; B. Cu, Al, Ni in 1 M HCl.

The comparison of Fig. 4.4A and Fig. 4.4B reveals that the amount of Al and Cu released from the Zr-BMG is on average 3-5 times higher than the dissolved amount of Zr and Nb. Whereas only about 1 ng cm^{-2} of Nb and 10 ng cm^{-2} of Zr were dissolved after 3 h of the corrosion attack, the concentrations of Al and Cu in the solution reached the level of 40-50 ng cm^{-2}. Ni dissolved to a level of about 20 ng cm^{-2} after 30 min of the corrosion attack, and then the signal remained stable within the next 2.5 h. Thus, all the constituents of $Zr_{58.5}Cu_{15.6}Ni_{12.8}Al_{10.3}Nb_{2.8}$ can be divided into tree groups based on their tendency to release: 1) Nb almost not dissolved; 2) Zr; 3) Al, Cu, (Ni).

Moreover, as it can be seen from Fig. 4.4, two stages of the corrosion attack can be clearly distinguished on the dissolution curves. A rapid release of all the elements with the exception of Nb was measured during the initial period of the corrosion attack (first 20-30 min). Later on, the corrosion behaviour of $Zr_{58.5}Cu_{15.6}Ni_{12.8}Al_{10.3}Nb_{2.8}$ was characterized by significantly reduced slopes of the dissolution curves.

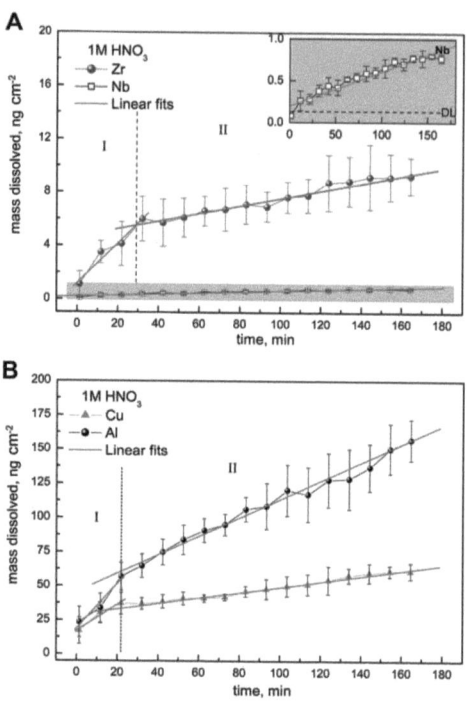

Fig. 4.5. Time-resolved dissolution rates of $Zr_{58.5}Cu_{15.6}Ni_{12.8}Al_{10.3}Nb_{2.8}$ constituent elements: A. Zr, Nb; B. Cu, Al, Ni in 1 M HNO_3.

The metal releases in 1M HNO_3 for (A) Zr, Nb; (B) Al, Cu under the open circuit conditions are presented in Fig. 4.5. The dissolution of Ni in nitric acid was below the detection limit. Generally, the same tendency of Al, Cu as compared to Zr, Nb dissolution was revealed. The distinct enhancement of Al dissolution was observed in Fig. 4.5B. After 3 h the concentration of Al in the nitric acid solution was equal to about 150 ng cm^{-2}. Cu and Zr were described by a slightly reduced dissolution rate as compared to release in HCl solution. The reason of the high Al release measured in the nitric acid is not yet fully understood, but the process of Al dissolution is probably related to the oxidizing nature of HNO_3. Although Al is tending to form a passive oxide layer, when immersed in nitric acid, a later XPS analysis of the oxide film formed on the surface of Zr-BMG reveals completely different composition and, hence, behaviour in nitric acid.

Dissolution curves for all the elements both in 1M HCl and 1M HNO_3 can be fitted using a linear regression equation according to $y = ax + b$, where a is the slope of the curve, which is equal to the dissolution rate and b is the intercept.

The quantitative data for the dissolution rates of Al, Cu, Ni, Zr and Nb for the initial 30 min (linear fit I for 0 to 30 min = LF I) and then for the next 2.5 h of the corrosion process (linear fit II for 30 to 180 min = LFII) are presented in Table 16. As it can be summarized from Table 16, the transition from region I (0 – 30 min of the corrosion attack) to region II (30 to 180 min of the corrosion attack) is accompanied by a 2-5 times reduction of the dissolution rates. High correlation coefficients $R^2 > 0.97$, calculated for linear fits of all the elements, prove the linear character of dissolution processes at stage II and point towards a constant corrosion rate. Overall, despite the usual high corrosivity of acids such as HCl and HNO_3, very low dissolution rates for all the elements were measured. The results are in good agreement with previous findings, when very low corrosion rates of 10^{-3} mm year^{-1} were determined for Nb-containing Zr-BMG based on static immersion tests [139].

An examination of the sample surface using SEM after the corrosion tests revealed a shiny surface with no distinct detectable sites of a corrosion initiation.

Thus, based on the quantitative results of the element-specific dissolution rates for the here studied Zr-BMG composition, the amount of dissolved species can not be predicted simply from the bulk metallic glass composition. Although, Zr is the main constituent element of $Zr_{58.5}Cu_{15.6}Ni_{12.8}Al_{10.3}Nb_{2.8}$, only relatively low concentrations of Zr were measured in the solution. In contrast, the preferential dissolution of Al and Cu was detected for both HCl and HNO_3 exposure.

Table 16. Element-resolved dissolution rates of $Zr_{58.5}Cu_{15.6}Ni_{12.8}Al_{10.3}Nb_{2.8}$ during exposure to 1 M HCl and 1M HNO_3 solutions.

Element		HCl		HNO_3	
		\multicolumn{4}{c}{$y = ax + b$}	
		dissolution rate (a), ng cm^{-2} min^{-1}	R^2	dissolution rate (a) ng cm^{-2} min^{-1}	R^2
Zr	LF I[a]	0.20 ± 0.07	0.9206	LF I	0.15 ± 0.02	0.9782
	LF II[b]	0.05 ± 0.01	0.9839	LF II	0.03 ± 0.01	0.9765
Nb	LFI+II	0.003 ± 0.001	0.9731	LFI+II	0.004 ± 0.0002	0.9612
Al	LF I	1.03 ± 0.46	0.9949	LF I	1.65 ± 0.74	0.9746
	LF II	0.23 ± 0.02	0.9899	LF II	0.68 ± 0.08	0.9934
Cu	LF I	0.75 ± 0.04	0.9987	LF I	0.95 ± 0.61	0.9802
	LF II	0.31 ± 0.03	0.9894	LF II	0.20 ± 0.03	0.9851
Ni	LF I	0.57 ± 0.10	0.9836	LF I	-	-
	LFII	-	-	LFII	-	-

[a] LF I – Linear fit of the dissolution curve at stage I; [b] LF II – Linear fit of the dissolution curve at stage II

It is known that the air exposed surfaces of Zr-bulk metallic glasses are covered with the thin protective oxide layer [12, 13]. Thus, the tendency of metals to dissolve from Zr-BMG can be most adequately explained based on the oxide film structure and composition. In the present study XPS analysis was employed before and after corrosion attack of $Zr_{58.5}Cu_{15.6}Ni_{12.8}Al_{10.3}Nb_{2.8}$ in 1M HCl to clarify the role of the oxide film in the corrosion behaviour of the bulk metallic glass. Fig. 4.6 shows the XPS spectra of Zr 3d, Nb 3d, Al 2s, Cu 2p, Ni 2p and O 1s after immersion in 1 M HCl solution for 16 h. The peaks of Zr $3d_{5/2}$ (182.2 eV) and Zr $3d_{3/2}$ (184.6 eV) were observed in the spectrum of Zr 3d, corresponding to Zr^{4+} oxidation state. The peaks at 178.3 eV and 180.5 eV were assigned to metallic Zr oxidation state (Zr^0) [12]. Nb 3d doublet spectrum consisted of Nb $3d_{3/2}$ (209.9 eV) and Nb $3d_{5/2}$ (207.1 eV), respectively, originating from Nb^{5+} [52]. The fitting of the overlapped Al 2s and Cu3s spectra was done for Al^{3+} (118.8eV), Al^0 (116.2 eV) and Cu 3s

(121.8eV) oxidation states [13]. The XPS spectrum of Cu 2p demonstrated peaks at 932.3 eV and 952.3 eV, which were assigned to Cu 2p3/2 and Cu 2p1/2, originating from Cu^{2+} state, respectively. In Ni 2p spectrum the peaks at 852.8 eV and 870.4 eV were assigned to Ni 2p3/2 and Ni 2p1/2, originating from Ni^{2+}. The O 1s spectrum is fitted by two peaks, at 530.3 eV and at 532.3 eV assigned to O^{2-} and to OH^-, respectively.

Table 17. Cationic composition (at. %) of the oxide film of $Zr_{58.5}Cu_{15.6}Ni_{12.8}Al_{10.3}Nb_{2.8}$ before and after exposure to 1 M HCl for 16 hours.

$Zr_{58.5}Cu_{15.6}Ni_{12.8}Al_{10.3}Nb_{2.8}$	polished Zr-BMG	Zr-BMG exposed to HCl (16 h)
Zr^{4+}	73.5 ± 0.8	76.5 ± 0.6
Zr^0	2.7 ± 0.3	2.4 ± 0.2
Nb^{5+}	4.6 ± 0.3	4.4 ± 0.1
Al^{3+}	12.0 ± 0.1	10.7 ± 0.8
Al^0	0	0.2 ± 0.1
Cu^{2+}	3.1 ± 0.4	2.4 ± 0.6
Ni^{2+}	4.2 ± 0.8	3.5 ± 0.4

The XPS derived cationic composition of the surface oxide film before and after immersion in hydrochloric acid is presented in Table 17. The results prove that all elements of the Zr-BMG are also present in the oxide layer, but in a different stoichiometric composition as compared to the composition of Zr-BMG itself. It can be concluded from Table 17 that the oxide film consists mainly from ZrO_2 with a smaller fraction of Al-oxide and very small amounts of Cu-, Nb- and Ni-oxides. Thus, the oxide layer is already enriched with Zr-oxide after the polishing procedure, probably leading to a high general corrosion resistance, due to the high chemical stability of ZrO_2.

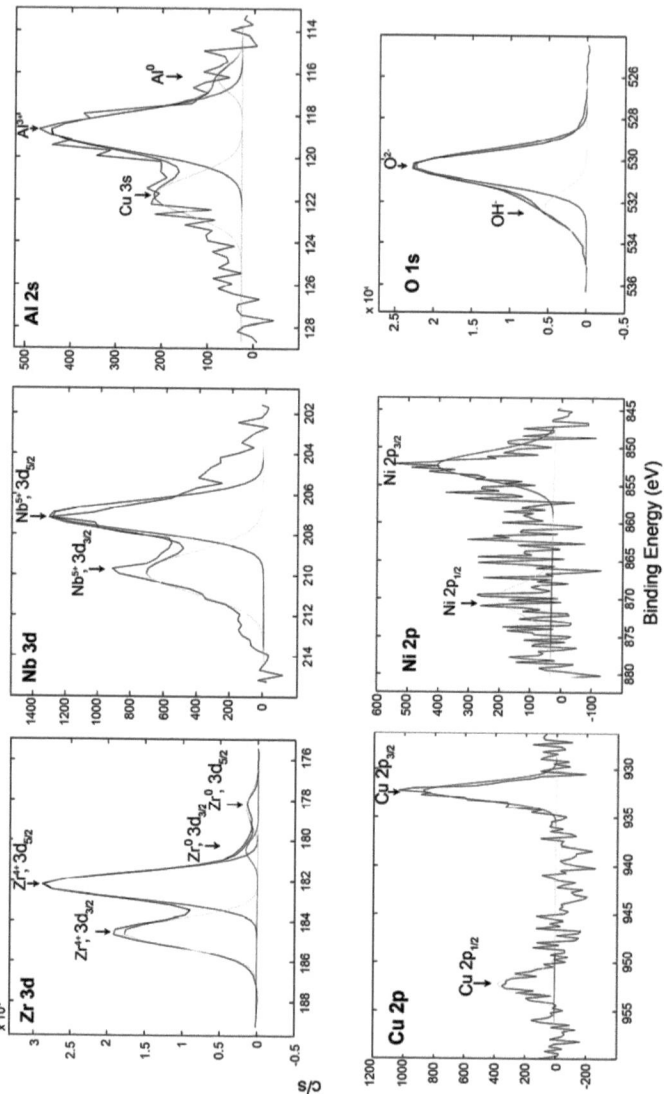

Fig. 4.6. XPS spectra of Zr 3d, Nb 3d, Al 2p, Cu 2p, Ni 2p and O 1s Zr58.5Cu15.6Ni12.8Al10.3Nb2.8 after exposure to 1 M HCl for 16 hours.

The XPS analysis also yielded 4.6 at. % of Nb-oxide in the surface film, an enriched content as compared to the composition of the here investigated Zr-BMG (2.8 at. %). It is known that Nb- and Zr-oxides possess a high corrosion resistance in a wide range of pHs [1]. Thus, if the oxide film formed on Zr-BMG is characterized by uniformity, a noble like behaviour can be expected even in acidic media.

Immersion in HCl solution leads to a further noticeable increase of the Zr^{4+} concentration in the surface film. At the same time the exposure in the acidic solution provokes the depletion of Al- and Cu-oxides in the film composition. These data are in good agreement with previous results of Hiromoto *et. al* [50, 51], who observed a depletion of Al in the oxide film upon polarization of Nb-free BMG $Zr_{65}Al_{7.5}Ni_{10}Cu_{17.5}$. Additionally, an increase of the open circuit potential was determined by Pang *et. al* [147] for $Zr_{60-x}Nb_xAl_{10}Ni_{10}Cu_{20}$ (x = 0-20 at. %), when immersing in 1 M HCl solution for the first hour of the corrosion attack. A fast initial increase of the open circuit potential was also detected for the BMG $Ti_{45}Zr_5Cu_{45}Ni_5$ with an immersion time of up to 1000 s [148]. These results indicated the improvement of the surface film stability during the corrosion attack. This improvement of the oxide can be explained based on the element-specific time-resolved data achieved with the microcapillary FI-ICP-MS.

The enrichment of the oxide film with Zr^{4+} content during corrosion attack can be most adequately explained by the following two reasons:

1. Selective dissolution of Al, Cu and Ni occurs at low pH, whereas valve metals like Zr and Nb tend only to a very slow dissolution process.

2. As assumed, the local concentrations of Zr^{4+} in the solution can reach the limit of solubility at the interface of oxide film and corrosive solution, thus provoking a re-precipitation of Zr-oxide. Consequently, the composition of the oxide layer shifts to the predominance of Zr-oxide.

The processes for Zr-oxide can be described by the following equations:

$$ZrO_2 + 4H^+ = Zr^{4+} + 2H_2O \tag{4.2}$$

or

$$ZrO_2 + (4-x) H^+ = Zr(OH)_x^{(4-x)+} + (2-x) H_2O \tag{4.3}$$

at low concentrations of Zr^{4+}.

Thus, the change in the slope of the dissolution curve observed for Al, Cu and Zr in Fig. 4.4 and Fig. 4.5 after about 30 min can be attributed to the online change in the composition and properties of the oxide film.

Based on the new time-resolved element-specific data achieved with a novel microcapillary FI-ICP-MS set-up, the processes, occurring at the interface of the corrosive liquid and the oxide film are schematically described in Fig. 4.7. The simultaneous processes of Al, Cu and Ni dissolution together with the enrichment of the oxide layer with Zr are proposed.

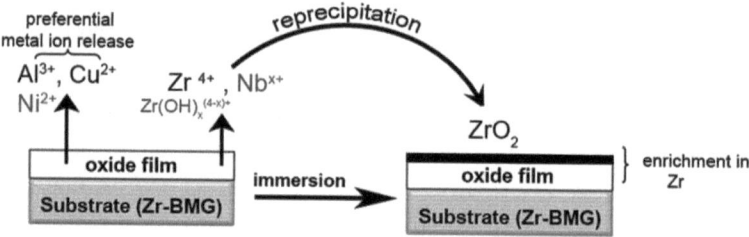

Fig. 4.6. Proposed mechanism of the dissolution processes occurring at the solid-liquid interface of Zr-BMG, when immersed in an acidic corrosive medium.

4.4. Conclusions.

It was proven that online microflow-capillary FI-ICP-MS set-up allows a transient and element-specific *in situ* investigation of corrosion processes of bulk metallic glasses with a high time resolution at a single sample spot. This is a significant advantage over

conventional static immersion tests, which are very time consuming and sample demanding, especially if the time-resolved analysis is required. The element-specific time-resolved *in situ* corrosion characteristics of $Zr_{58.5}Cu_{15.6}Ni_{12.8}Al_{10.3}Nb_{2.8}$ were studied for the first time with the microflow-capillary FI-ICP-MS technique in 1M HCl and 1 M HNO_3. The investigation revealed that the multi-element release of Zr-BMG follows a clear two-step process, with an initial stage of 20-30 min followed by a significantly reduced dissolution rate. A preferential dissolution of Cu and Al from the oxide film was observed together with the simultaneous enrichment of Zr-oxide content in the film. The high corrosion resistance after the initial phase was attributed to the elemental composition change in the oxide film.

5. Online hyphenation of potentiostat to a microflow-capillary FI-ICP-MS for simultaneous *in situ* electrochemical, time and element resolved characterization of local corrosion processes - An application for Zr-bulk metallic glass.

(*N. Homazava, T. Suter, P. Schmutz, S. Toggweiler, A. Grimberg, U. Krähenbühl, A. Ulrich, Online hyphenation of potentiostat to a microflow-capillary FI-ICP-MS for simultaneous in situ electrochemical, time and element resolved characterization of local corrosion processes - An application for Zr-bulk metallic glass, Journal of Analytical Atomic Spectrometry 24 (2009) 1161-1169 [149].)*

5.1. Overview.

So far, only measurements at open circuit potential were available with the microflow-capillary FI-ICP-MS set-up. In this Chapter, a hyphenation of an electrochemical control to the microflow-capillary FI-ICP-MS set-up is presented, allowing simultaneous online ICP-MS and electrochemical data monitoring during the corrosion process. This opens new possibilities in corrosion studies by enabling simultaneous electrochemical and element-specific data acquisition. The idea is realized using the investigated sample as the working electrode, while the reference and counter micro-electrodes are installed into the microflow-capillary. Moreover, a further capillary downsizing, especially for highly corrosion resistant materials like BMG, requires additional electrochemical polarization to achieve measurable dissolution rates.

The efficiency of this hyphenated technique is verified by a corrosion study on Zr-bulk metallic glass with the composition of $Zr_{58.5}Cu_{15.6}Ni_{12.8}Al_{10.3}Nb_{2.8}$. In Chapter 4 element-resolved dissolution behaviour of $Zr_{58.5}Cu_{15.6}Ni_{12.8}Al_{10.3}Nb_{2.8}$ with the microflow-capillary FI-ICP-MS at open circuit potential only was investigated. An additional hyphenation of the electrochemical control allows the simultaneous characterization of Zr-BMG corrosion behaviour with both element-specific and electrochemical techniques, which is so far not accessible in the literature. The corrosion susceptibility of $Zr_{58.5}Cu_{15.6}Ni_{12.8}Al_{10.3}Nb_{2.8}$ in 0.1 M HCl, 0.1 M NaCl and 0.001 M NaCl was evaluated at open circuit potential and during electrochemical potentiodynamic polarization of the sample surface. Additionally, the Zr-BMG surface before and after corrosion attack was characterized by scanning electron microscopy with energy dispersive x-ray spectrometry.

5.2. Experimental.

5.2.1. Microflow-capillary FI-ICP-MS set-up coupled with the electrochemical control.

The microflow-capillary used in the presented study has an internal diameter of 800 µm. The electrolyte inside the microflow-capillary was pumped with a cycling flow rate of 500 µl min^{-1}. The total cycling volume of the electrolyte was equal to 620µl, whereas aliquots of 20 µl only were transiently introduced into ICP-MS using a small flow injection loop. The elements released from the material during corrosion were detected online using a quadrupole inductively coupled plasma mass spectrometer ICP-MS ELAN 6000. The details of the instrument operation conditions are presented in Table 18. The online ICP-MS analysis was performed every 115 s during the potentiodynamic polarization of the sample.

To achieve a simultaneous acquisition of the ICP-MS and potentiodynamic polarization data a high resolution, low noise measuring system was coupled to the microflow-capillary FI-ICP-MS set-up. A modified low-noise battery operated potentiostat (Jaissle 1002T-NC-3) was used for the electrochemical measurements. The input resistance was better than 10^{15} Ω and the input current about 10^{-14} A (20°C). In combination with a good shielding, corrosion currents as low as 10 fA (10^{-14} A) could be detected. A three electrode cell concept with a silver/silver chloride (Ag/AgCl) reference electrode (Dri-Ref 450, World Precision Instruments, Sarasota, FL, USA) and a platinum wire (99.95%, World Precision Instruments, Sarasota, FL, USA) as counter electrode was used. The sample served as a working electrode.

Table 18. ICP-MS instrument operation conditions

ICP-MS Instrument	ELAN 6000
Sample introduction system	Micromist nebulizer MMN 100 with Cinnabar spray chamber
Sampling and skimmer cones	Nickel

Plasma parameters	
Rf Power (W)	1100
Coolant gas flow-rate (L min^{-1})	15
Auxiliary gas flow-rate (L min^{-1})	1
Nebulizer gas flow-rate (L min^{-1})	0.96
Data acquisition parameters	
Dwell time (ms)	30
Readings per replicate	250
Number of replicates	15-20
Analytes monitored	$^{27}Al^+$, $^{60}Ni^+$, $^{65}Cu^+$, $^{90}Zr^+$, $^{93}Nb^+$

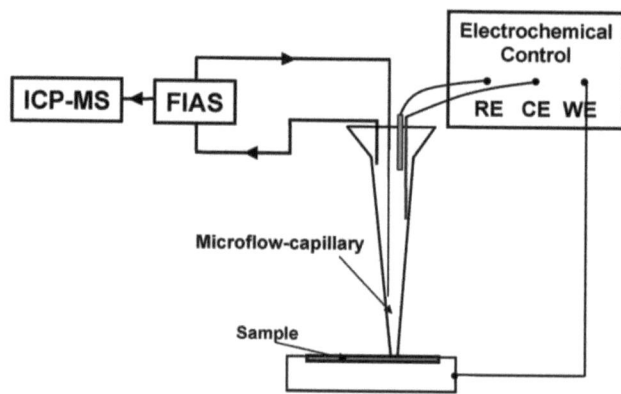

Fig. 5.1. Scheme of an adaptation of the electrochemical control to the microflow-capillary FI-ICP-MS set-up.

The reference and counter electrodes were inserted into the microflow-capillary. Fig. 5.1 schematically shows an adaptation of the electrochemical control to the microflow-capillary FI-ICP-MS set-up.

Since the physical dimensions of the electrodes installed inside the capillary are critical, electrodes with smallest diameters available were implemented. The Pt wire had a diameter of 250 µm, whereas the diameter of the reference micro-electrode tip was 450 µm. Prior the installation, the electrodes were leached in 1 M hydrochloric acid to minimize a contamination of the corrosive medium. The potentiodynamic polarization measurements were operated with a scanning rate of 0.5 mV s^{-1} from -400 mV to +1000 mV (vs Ag/AgCl) after initial immersion at open circuit potential for 5 min. Simultaneously ICP-MS data was acquired every 115 s.

5.2.2. SEM-EDX.

The surface of the freshly polished sample before corrosion attack and the corroded sample after the anodic polarization up to +1000 mV (vs. Ag/AgCl) was studied using a Hitachi S-4800 scanning electron microscope equipped with an Oxford energy dispersive X-ray spectrometer. The SEM images were recorded using 5 to 10 keV electron beam energy and a sample distance of 8 mm.

5.2.3. Materials and chemicals.

The Zr-BMG investigated had a composition of $Zr_{58.5}Cu_{15.6}Ni_{12.8}Al_{10.3}Nb_{2.8}$. The sample was first ground with a SiC paper down to 4000 grit and then polished with a diamond paste down to 1 µm. The surface of the polished sample was cleaned in an ultrasonic bath with absolute ethanol (99.8%, pro analysis quality, Merck, Germany). All corrosion investigations were performed on a freshly polished sample at room temperature.

The following solutions were used as corrosive media: 0.1 M HCl, 0.1 M NaCl and 0.001 M NaCl. The 0.1 M HCl solution was prepared from concentrated hydrochloric acid of ultrapure quality (Merck, Germany). The 0.1 M and 0.001 M NaCl solutions were prepared from sodium chloride of suprapur quality (99.99%, Merck, Germany).

Single element stock solutions of Zr, Nb, Cu, Al and Ni of ICP-MS quality (1 g L^{-1}, Merck, Germany) were step-wise diluted to prepare single element standard solutions for calibration. The ICP-MS calibration procedure was performed using the mentioned single element standard solutions with matrix matching due to the applied corrosion media, *i.e.* each standard solution contained 0.1 M HCl, 0.1 M NaCl or 0.001 M NaCl as a matrix.

5.3. Results and discussion.

5.3.1. Hyphenation of the potentiostat to the microflow-capillary FI-ICP-MS set-up. Analytical optimization procedure.

To allow simultaneous electrochemical and element-resolved data acquisition during corrosion of the Zr-BMG, a potentiostat was coupled to the microflow-capillary FI-ICP-MS set-up. The Zr-BMG was connected to the potentiostat instrument as a working electrode. Pt-wire and Ag/AgCl electrodes were inserted into the microcapillary as counter and reference electrodes, respectively.

The counter electrode (CE) and reference electrode (RE) have to fulfil the following criteria to be appropriate for use in the current microflow-capillary set-up:

a) to be equipped with the smallest electrode dimensions;

b) to provide minimal contamination levels to the corrosive medium.

Both electrodes were preliminary leached in the different relevant corrosion media solutions to estimate the possible contamination levels, which may originate from the electrodes.

Fig. 5.2A shows the results of the static RE and CE leach-out in 0.1 M NaCl, 0.1 M HCl and 1 M HCl. The electrodes were immersed in the mentioned solutions for 3 h; the solutions were later on analyzed with ICP-MS. Fig. 5.2B demonstrates the results of the dynamic leaching of the RE and CE together in 1M HCl. In this case the electrodes were inserted into the capillary filled with 1M HCl solution, which was pumped with a cycling flow of 500 $\mu l \ min^{-1}$ for 2 h according to the subsequent corrosion experiments. The same elements as in the static leaching were monitored. However, only for the elements Al, Mg, and Zn significant signals have been detected.

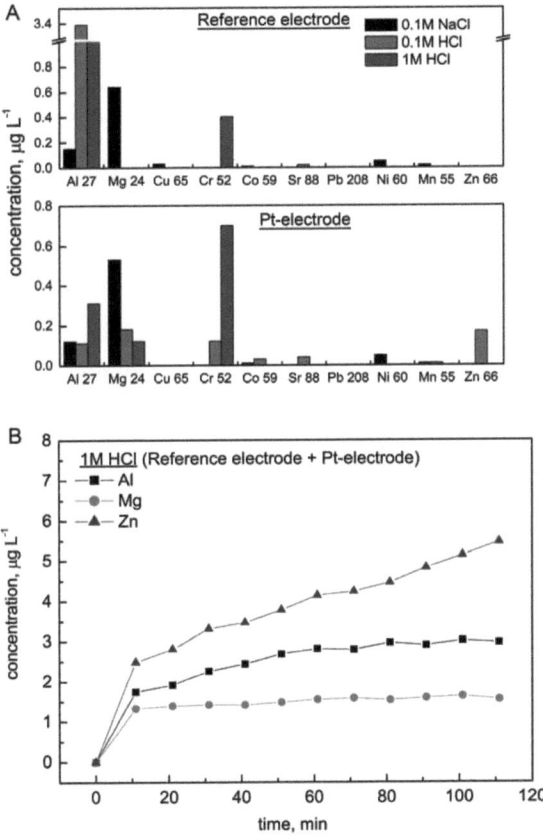

Fig. 5.2. A. Elemental concentrations in 0.1 M NaCl, 0.1 M HCl and 1 M HCl solutions after the static leaching procedure of Pt-electrode and Ag/AgCl Dri-Ref reference electrodes; B. Elemental concentrations in 1 M HCl solution after dynamic leaching of Pt-electrode and Ag/AgCl Dri-Ref reference electrode together.

As it can be concluded from Fig. 5.2A and Fig. 5.2B the highest contamination levels were detected for Al and Mg at levels of 1-3 µg L^{-1}. The increased signal level for Cr in HCl solution originating from ArCl$^+$ spectral interferences was compensated by matrix matching of blank solution and standards.

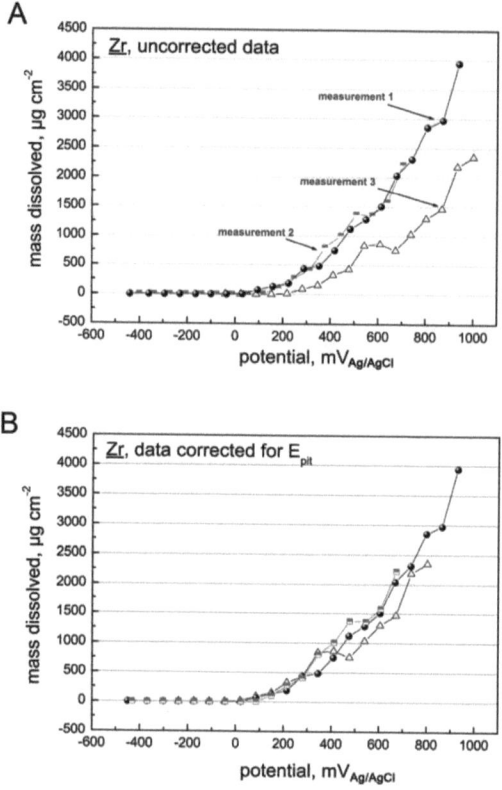

Fig. 5.3. Correction of the ICP-MS measurements according to different values of E_{pit} for 3 independent corrosion measurements of Zr in 0.1 M NaCl: A. Non-corrected data; B. Corrected data.

To avoid contamination of corrosive media used in the corrosion experiments, both electrodes were preliminary leached in 1 M HCl for 3 hours and several times rinsed with ultra-pure Milli-Q water before they were installed into the microflow-capillary. During the first 5 min of the corrosion investigation, the ICP-MS background signal was monitored at open circuit potential. Later on it was used as a blank level for the procedure of the ICP-MS signal calculation.

The detection limits of the technique for the elements of interest $^{27}Al^+$, $^{60}Ni^+$, $^{65}Cu^+$, $^{90}Zr^+$ and $^{93}Nb^+$ were estimated on a level of ng L^{-1} and are presented in the Chapter 4. Each corrosion investigation was repeated three times at random spots of the Zr-BMG sample. The standard deviations (SDs) of the element concentration determination, originating from the ICP-MS analysis were much lower compared to the SDs of the determined element concentrations originating from these triple determinations at different spots. Hence, the precision of the technique is limited by the SDs of the multiple determinations.

Moreover, the ICP-MS data acquired in the measurements are corrected for the value of the pitting potential (E_{pit}, electrochemical data) for each measurement. Fig. 5.3 shows an exemplary procedure of the ICP-MS Zr data correction for E_{pit} for three independent corrosion measurements in 0.1 M NaCl. A comparison of Fig. 5.3A and Fig. 5.3B reveals that the mentioned correction procedure leads to final data with increased precision.

5.3.2. Corrosion study on $Zr_{58.5}Cu_{15.6}Ni_{12.8}Al_{10.3}Nb_{2.8}$. Potentiodynamic polarization.

Potentiodynamic polarization curves obtained for $Zr_{58.5}Cu_{15.6}Ni_{12.8}Al_{10.3}Nb_{2.8}$ in 0.1 M NaCl, 0.001 M NaCl and 0.1 M HCl are shown in Fig. 5.4. The open circuit potential (E_{ocp}) and the pitting potential (E_{pit}) shift towards more negative values, when the acidity of the corrosive medium or the chloride concentration is increased. These results are in the following ranking:

$$E_{pit}\ (0.1\ M\ HCl) < E_{pit}\ (0.1\ M\ NaCl) < E_{pit}\ (0.001\ M\ NaCl)$$

The polarization curve of Zr-BMG in 0.001 M NaCl is characterized by the presence of a wide passive region, $\Delta E = E_{pit} - E_{ocp} = 285$ mV (*vs* Ag/AgCl), whereas for a higher chloride concentration the passive region is much more narrow, $\Delta E = 71$ mV (*vs* Ag/AgCl) for 0.1 M NaCl. In 0.1 M HCl, there is a first region of $\Delta E = 50$ mV (*vs* Ag/AgCl) with lower dissolution rate, but no real passivation is observed. $Zr_{58.5}Cu_{15.6}Ni_{12.8}Al_{10.3}Nb_{2.8}$ exhibits a high uniform corrosion resistance indicated by low values of passive current density on a level of 10^{-7}-10^{-6} A cm^{-2} for the corrosive media tested in the neutral pH domain.

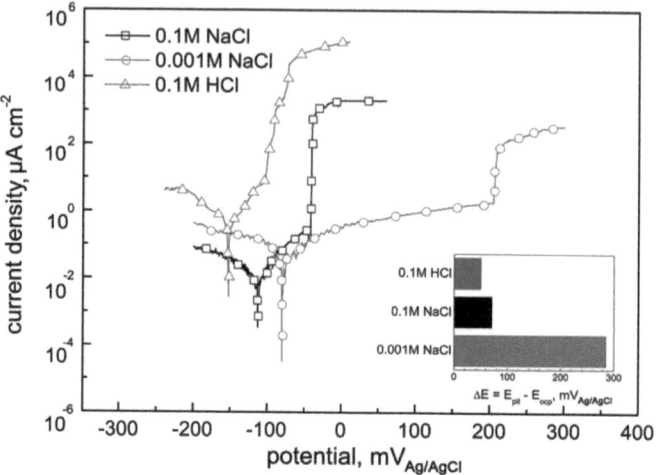

Fig. 5.4. Potentiodynamic polarization curves of $Zr_{58.5}Cu_{15.6}Ni_{12.8}Al_{10.3}Nb_{2.8}$ in 0.1 M NaCl, 0.001 M NaCl and 0.1 M HCl.

However, during anodic polarization in chloride containing solutions, the Zr-BMG is highly prone to localized (pitting) corrosion. These findings are consistent with electrochemical results previously published for Zr-BMGs of other compositions [150, 151].

Based on the potentiodynamic polarization data, conclusions on the corrosion resistance or susceptibility of Zr-BMG can be made. However, an important additional element-resolved characterization of Zr-BMG corrosion dissolution behaviour is only accessible using the novel potentiostat hyphenated microflow-capillary FI-ICP-MS set-up.

5.3.3. Corrosion study on $Zr_{58.5}Cu_{15.6}Ni_{12.8}Al_{10.3}Nb_{2.8}$. Element- and time resolved online dissolution behaviour monitored with FI-ICP-MS technique under electrochemical control.

Fig. 5.5A-E shows the measured elemental dissolution rates of $Zr_{58.5}Cu_{15.6}Ni_{12.8}Al_{10.3}Nb_{2.8}$ in 0.1 M NaCl, 0.001 M NaCl and 0.1 M HCl at different potentials achieved during the potentiodynamic polarization of the sample. For all elements monitored with ICP-MS the dissolution curve can be easily divided into two regions before and after pitting potential. The values of the pitting potentials in 0.1 M NaCl, 0.001 M NaCl and 0.1 M HCl are exemplary marked on the Zr-dissolution curve (Fig. 5.5A). Before the pitting potential is reached, only very low Al and Cu concentrations in the range of 20 to 60 ng cm^{-2} are detected for all investigated corrosion media.

For the elements Zr, Nb and Ni, the ICP-MS signals remain almost at background level until the potentiodynamic polarization scan reaches the pitting potential value. The low concentrations of Al and Cu are already detected during cathodic prepolarization of the sample and at open circuit potential immersion prior the anodic polarization, *e.g.* at potentials from -400 to -100 mV (*vs* Ag/AgCl). Thus, the initial process of Al and Cu release from the Zr-BMG into corrosive solution can be explained as a process of chemical dissolution of the natural oxide film, when alkalisation of the solution at the surface occurs as a result of cathodic reduction. Natural oxide films (called passive films) are usually formed on top of the bulk metallic glasses at ambient air and have a typical thickness of 5-10 nm [12]. A similar mechanism of Zr-BMG oxide film dissolution at open circuit potential was proposed in the previous Chapter.

As the potentiodynamic polarization curve passes through the value of E_{pit} (onset of localized corrosion) a massive release of all elements is detected online with ICP-MS. The steepness of the dissolution curve decreases in the following order

0.1M HCl > 0.1 M NaCl > 0.001 M NaCl,

confirming the electrochemical data of $Zr_{58.5}Cu_{15.6}Ni_{12.8}Al_{10.3}Nb_{2.8}$ corrosion susceptibility.

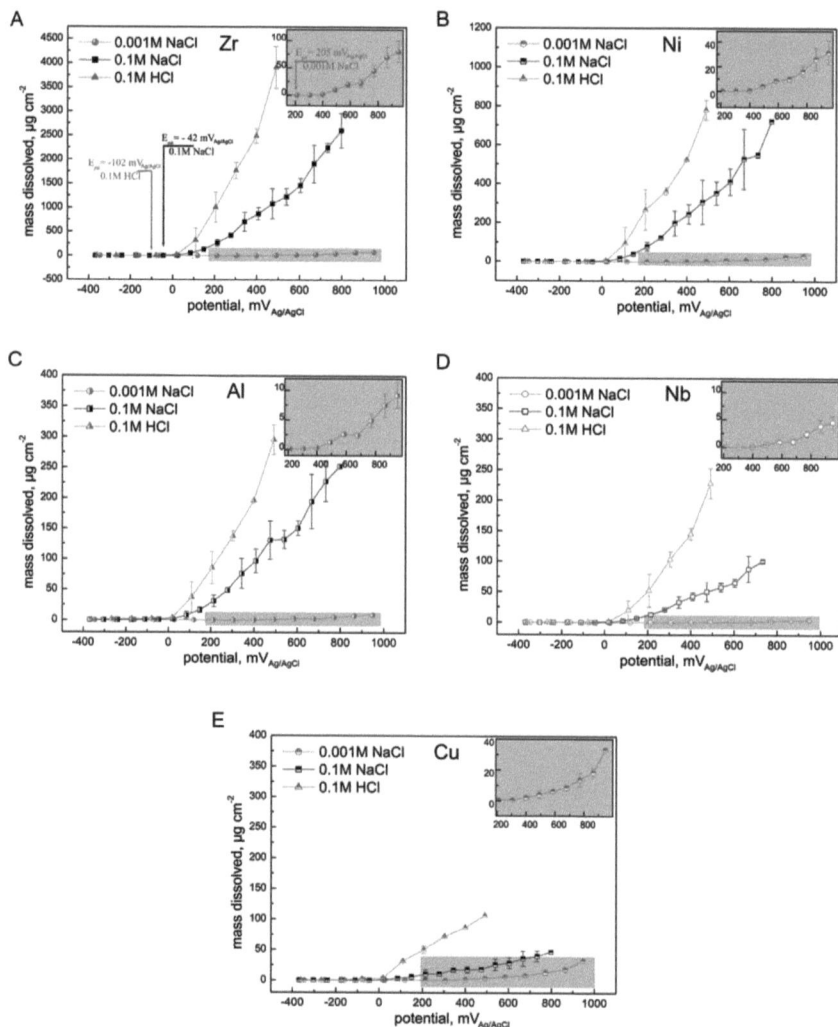

Fig. 5.5. Dissolution behaviour of $Zr_{58.5}Cu_{15.6}Ni_{12.8}Al_{10.3}Nb_{2.8}$ constituent elements upon potentiodynamic polarization: A. zirconium Zr; B. nickel Ni; C. aluminium Al; D. niobium Nb; E. copper Cu.

The absolute amount of Zr released in 0.1 M HCl and 0.1 M NaCl is estimated in the range of mg cm^{-2}, whereas for all other elements the amount of species dissolved is in the range of µg cm^{-2}. Generally, the amount of species released in 0.1 M HCl is 3 to 5 times higher than in 0.1 M NaCl. The dissolution behaviour in the lower chloride concentrated 0.001 M NaCl is characterized by significantly reduced dissolution rates. On average the dissolved mass is 30 to 40 times lower than in 0.1 M NaCl. The trends are also consistent with the limiting current density measured electrochemically that is much higher for HCl than for the NaCl solution.

The element-resolved dissolution rates for $Zr_{58.5}Cu_{15.6}Ni_{12.8}Al_{10.3}Nb_{2.8}$ decrease in the following order, based on the data shown in Fig. 5.5A to Fig. 5.5E:

$$Zr > Ni > Al > Nb > Cu.$$

Comparing this data set to the mass composition of the BMG material (70.06 % Zr, 13.01 % Cu, 9.86 % Ni, 3.65 % Al, and 3.42 % Nb) it can be concluded that:

a) the release of all elements with the exception of Cu is in agreement with the composition of the bulk metallic glass;

b) the release of Cu from $Zr_{58.5}Cu_{15.6}Ni_{12.8}Al_{10.3}Nb_{2.8}$ is strongly inhibited.

The dependence of the mass ratio of elements dissolved in 0.1 M HCl, 0.1 M NaCl and 0.001 M NaCl compared to the nominal mass ratio of elements derived from the Zr-BMG composition is shown in Fig. 5.6A to Fig. 5.6D. Fig. 5.6A and Fig. 5.6D indicate preferential Al and Ni dissolution, characterized by two times higher mass ratios of Al to Zr and Ni to Zr dissolved from the material compared to the nominal composition ratios in all corrosive media. Nb and Zr are released very close to the nominal ratio in 0.1 M HCl, 0.1 M NaCl and 0.001 M NaCl, indicating that the dissolution of Zr and Nb proceeds in accordance with the material composition (Fig. 5.6B). The ratio of Cu to Zr dissolved from the material is strongly reduced especially in the high chloride concentrated solutions (0.1 M HCl and 0.1 M NaCl), whereas for 0.001 M NaCl an enhanced Cu/Zr ratio is detected (Fig. 5.6C).

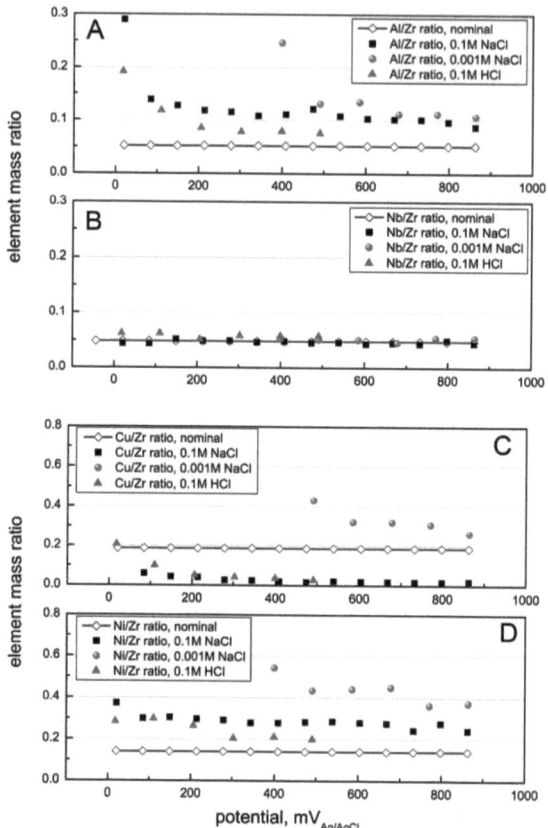

Fig. 5.6. The dependence of the mass ratio of elements dissolved in 0.1 M HCl, 0.1 M NaCl and 0.001 M NaCl compared to the nominal mass ratio of elements derived from the Zr-BMG composition: A. Al/Zr ratios; B. Nb/Zr ratios; C. Cu/Zr ratios; D. Ni/Zr ratios.

It is important to point out that only a relative enhancement of the Cu/Zr ratio in 0.001 M NaCl is observed, the absolute amount of copper dissolved from the material follows the same sequence as for the other elements:

$$0.1\ M\ HCl > 0.1\ M\ NaCl > 0.001\ M\ NaCl$$

The following explanation of the observed data is proposed. The elements of the Zr-BMG are characterized by standard electrode potentials: $E°$ (Zr^{4+}/Zr) = -1.45 V (*vs* SCE); $E°$ (Nb^{3+}/Nb) = -1.099 V (*vs* SCE); $E°$ (Al^{3+}/Al) = -1.662 V (*vs* SCE); $E°$ (Ni^{2+}/Ni) = -0.257 V (*vs* SCE); $E°$ (Cu^{2+}/Cu) = +0.342 V (*vs* SCE) [152]. Thus, the active dissolution processes for all elements, with the exception of Cu, can be expected after oxide film breakdown and as soon as the E_{pit} is reached. However, the standard electrode potential is related to the binding energy of a compound, meaning that for a Zr-BMG comparison of single elements data is only indicative. The increased dissolution rates of Al and Ni compared to Nb and Zr can be interpreted if the solubility of the corrosion products is taken into account. Nb chloride has a low solubility in both neutral and acidic aqueous solution and tends to a fast hydrolysis process, which can be described as follows:

$$NbCl_5 + xH_2O \rightarrow Nb(OH)_xCl_{5-x} + xH^+ + xCl^- \quad (5.1)$$

At chloride concentrations lower than 2M a formation of a flocculent precipitate of $Nb(OH)_3Cl_2$ and/or $Nb(OH)_5$ occurs [153].

Zr chloride is also characterized by a low solubility in neutral and weak acidic aqueous solutions, resulting in a similar hydrolysis process [154]:

$$Zr^{4+} + xH_2O \rightarrow Zr(OH)_x^{(4-x)+} + xH^+ \quad (5.2)$$

Hence, the precipitation of Zr and Nb hydrolyzed corrosion products is expected in the studied corrosive media. On the other hand, Al and Ni chlorides have a high solubility in both neutral and acidic solutions. Therefore, an enhanced dissolution of Al and Ni compared to Zr and Nb is explainable by the different solubility products of these elements.

Due to the highest standard electrode potential of Cu ($E°$ (Cu^{2+}/Cu) = +0.342 V (*vs* SCE)) among all elements in $Zr_{58.5}Cu_{15.6}Ni_{12.8}Al_{10.3}Nb_{2.8}$, a noble behaviour of Cu is expected and the lowest dissolution rate for Cu is reasonable. But here again, first, preferential dissolution steps need to occur, to be able to speak of pure copper dissolution. Furthermore, the increased ratio of Cu/Zr release in 0.001 M NaCl is yet not fully understood. However, studies of localized corrosion behaviour of copper indicate that its susceptibility and dissolution is influenced by the formation of a poorly soluble CuCl compounds. The precipitate can only form in presence of large amount of chloride, and this support the fact that highest susceptibility to localized corrosion for copper is found for 0.001 M NaCl [155]. Localized corrosion of copper is however only occurs at pH's above 8 so that the explanation needs to be investigated in more detail. However, dealloying and copper remnant are often found, when copper containing compounds are considered [156].

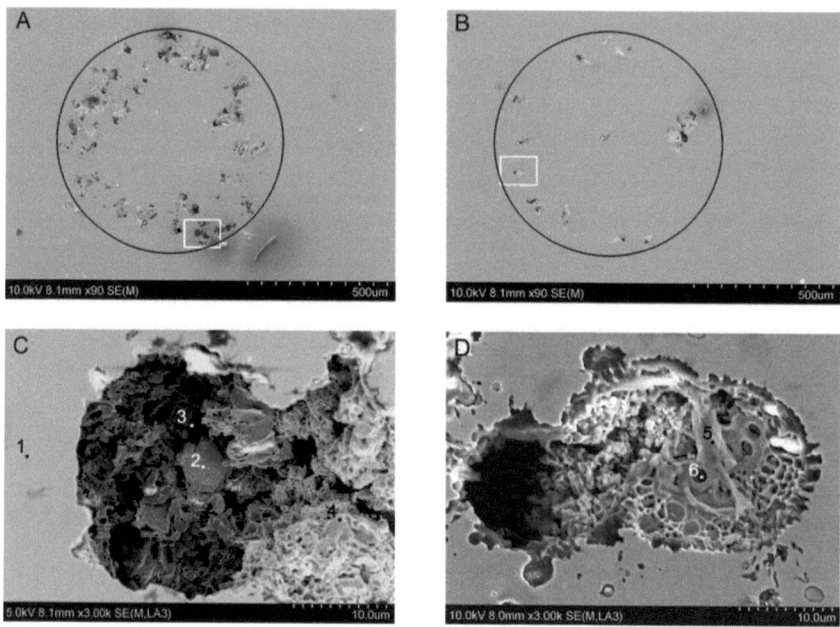

Fig. 5.7. SEM images of the corroded surface of Zr-BMG after potentiodynamic polarization up to +1000 mV (*vs* Ag/AgCl) in: A. 0.1 M HCl; B. 0.1 M NaCl. SEM images of the pits on the surface of Zr-BMG in: C. 0.1 M HCl (enlarged section of Fig. 5.7A); D. 0.1 M NaCl (enlarged section of Fig. 5.7B). The numbered points indicate the spots, where the EDX analysis is performed.

To discuss the data presented in this Chapter, the morphology of the pits formed on the surface of Zr-BMG after anodic polarization up to +1000 mV (*vs* Ag/AgCl) was studied with SEM-EDX and are provided in Fig. 5.7A and Fig. 5.7B. Both figures show overviews of the corroded area, pits growth occurred in the area where the capillary was placed (a dark circle with a radius of about 400 µm). Detailed images of the pits formed in 0.1 M HCl and 0.1 M NaCl are shown in Fig. 5.7C and Fig. 5.7D, respectively. It is clearly visible that the number and the pit size are higher in 0.1 M HCl. Remarkable is the shape of the corrosion attack at the Zr-BMG surface, which appears in form of a circle of about 800 µm, whereas the inner region seems to be less attacked. The exact reason for this phenomenon is not yet understood. A possible explanation might be a local enhancement of acidity or chloride concentration at the outer region, caused by less well mixing zones and diffusion problems due to the capillary geometry or crevices under the capillary. This can obviously play a role when fast active dissolution takes place, but in the presented case also the corrosion initiation is dependent on the location. This observation also points on an another possible cause, which is the pressure applied on the surface by the capillary and which is higher close to the capillary walls than in the middle of the exposed area. Induced stress has to be taken into account when the susceptibility to localized corrosion initiation of thin passive film is considered.

The results of the EDX analysis performed for the points indicated by numbers in Fig. 5.7C and Fig. 5.7D are given in Table 19. The EDX analysis of point 1 in the gray area of Fig. 5.7C provides a composition, which is quite close to the nominal composition of the material, thus it is related to the non-corroded sample surface. However, by EDX analysis the Nb signal could not be detected, which is surprising because although the Nb concentration is small, it should still be above the detection limit of EDX. The points 2 and 3 located in the centre of a pit formed in 0.1 M HCl show a high enrichment of Cu inside the pit but no evidence of thick corrosion products on the surface. The EDX analysis of the outer region of the pit (point 4 in Fig. 5.7C) reveals increased oxygen content, confirming the formation of corrosion products for this area. The EDX analysis performed on the corroded surface of Zr-BMG in 0.1 M NaCl provides similar results, *i.e.* enrichment of Cu in the centre of the pit (point 6 in Fig. 5.7D).

Table 19. Mass concentrations of elements in numbered spots (Fig. 5.7) derived from EDX analysis at the marked points in the Fig. 5.7C and Fig. 5.7D.

	O	Al	Ni	Cu	Zr	Nb
Nominal composition	-	3.65	9.86	13.01	70.06	3.42
Point 1	-	3.6	8.8	12.9	74.7	-
Point 2	-	-	-	86.0	14.0	-
Point 3	-	-	-	83.9	16.1	-
Point 4	6.8	2.0	8.8	29.8	52.6	-
Point 5	11.4	-	13.0	41.3	34.3	-
Point 6	-	-	17.2	67.3	15.5	-

Thus, the results of SEM-EDX analysis confirm the data achieved with the novel potentiostat hyphenated microflow-capillary FI-ICP-MS technique. A preferential active dissolution of less noble elements like Zr and Al and an enrichment of Cu inside the pits was also proposed for Zr-based bulk metallic glasses of different compositions, *e.g.* for $Zr_{50}Cu_{(40-x)}Al_{10}Pd_x$ [157] or Cu-Zr metallic glasses [158]. The ICP-MS observation also points that the role of Zr is limited to its passivation properties. Thus, the data achieved with the novel potentiostat hyphenated microflow-capillary FI-ICP-MS technique clearly demonstrate a preferential dissolution of less noble elements like Ni and Al from Zr-BMG, whereas Cu release from the material is strongly hindered.

5.4. Conclusions.

The hyphenation of the electrochemical control to the microflow-capillary FI-ICP-MS technique offers distinct advantages over traditional separate electrochemical techniques or chemical bulk immersion tests by plasma spectrometry. Due to the adaptation of the electrochemical instrument a control of the corrosion processes can be achieved. At the same time a simultaneous acquisition of electrochemical and online time- and element-resolved ICP-MS data allows a thorough online characterization of corrosion behaviour of an investigated material.

The efficiency of the hyphenated technique was demonstrated by analysis of the corrosion susceptibility of $Zr_{58.5}Cu_{15.6}Ni_{12.8}Al_{10.3}Nb_{2.8}$ in 0.1 M HCl, 0.1 M NaCl and 0.001 M NaCl solutions. The electrochemical and element-resolved corrosion behaviour was investigated during potentiodynamic polarization of the bulk metallic glass sample from -400 mV to +1000 mV (*vs* Ag/AgCl).

The analysis revealed a very low dissolution of Al and Cu on a level of ng cm^{-2} in the cathodic domain. This finding is explained by a preferential process of Al and Cu dissolution from the oxide film as a result of alkalinisation at the sample surface. During the polarization of the sample, once the E_{pit} is reached, a massive release of all elements (with the exception of Cu) is detected in the range of μg cm^{-2} to mg cm^{-2}. The element-resolved dissolution rates of the elements from the bulk metallic glass decreases in the following order: Zr > Ni > Al > Nb > Cu.

Chapter 5

6. Summary and outlook.

Within the scope of the PhD thesis a novel analytical technique for online *in situ* element-specific and time-resolved investigation of corrosion processes was developed. The microflow-capillary set-up suitable for ultra-trace multi-element corrosion analysis was constructed and coupled online to an ICP-MS instrument using flow injection sample introduction system. Moreover, as a final step of the technique improvement, an electrochemical control was hyphenated to the set-up allowing simultaneous chemical and electrochemical data acquisition.

The development of the microflow-capillary FI-ICP-MS technique included the development of a suitable microflow-capillary and strategies for contamination-minimized chemical ultra-trace analysis. Moreover, concepts for the analysis of high salt matrix corrosion samples and appropriate methods for the analysis of low liquid sample volumes (20-100 µl) using an alternative ICP-MS sample introduction system.

The efficiency of the novel analytical technique was demonstrated by corrosion investigation of commercially relevant samples in comparison to other independent analytical methods typically used in corrosion science (*e.g.* SEM-EDX, XPS).

1. Online *in situ* corrosion characterization of several industrially used Al alloys, *e.g.* AA 5050, AA 5754 and AA 6111 was performed with the novel technique. The element- and time-resolved dissolution behaviour was studied as a function of different experimental parameters, including the type and concentration of the corrosive medium, pH value *etc*. The detection limits were found to be at extremely low levels of about 0.01-0.06 µg cm^{-2} which allowed element-specific corrosion investigations not only for the main alloying elements but also a quantification of secondary alloying element release, *e.g.* Fe, Mn or Cu.

2. Corrosion susceptibility characteristics of Zr-bulk metallic glass ($Zr_{58.5}Cu_{15.6}Ni_{12.8}Al_{10.3}Nb_{2.8}$) were studied providing the new previously not available data on element-resolved online dissolution behaviour in different corrosive media (1 M HNO_3, 1 M HCl, 0.1 M HCl, 0.1 M NaCl, 0.001 M NaCl). Moreover, the data achieved with the chemical ICP-MS analysis were compared to the simultaneously acquired electrochemical potentiodynamic polarization data.

Summary and Outlook

The developed microflow-capillary FI-ICP-MS technique coupled with an electrochemical control provides essentially new important data related to the solution chemistry, which is established during local surface degradation processes. In future, this information can be used for reliable modelling of complex corrosion processes and mechanisms for metallic and non-metallic materials.

As an outlook further improvement and optimization steps in the technique development should be mentioned:

1. Improvement of the current microflow-capillary FI-ICP-MS set-up in terms of automated calibration and internal standardization procedures.

2. Adding and mixing of an internal standard to improve signal stability.

3. Concepts for interference correction of isobaric or polyatomic overlaps.

4. Tracer experiments to estimate mixing capabilities of a specific capillary design. Therefore, stable tracer elements should be added to the circulating corrosive medium in the microflow-capillary. The initial corrosive medium is tracer-free. The time-dependent depletion of the tracer concentration is determined by ICP-MS. The mixing capabilities can be evaluated, comparing the measured tracer depletion to the calculated one. Fig. 6.1 shows first results of the tracer-experiments, using Rh 10 µg L^{-1} as a stable, internal element tracer.

5. Based on the data of the tracer experiments for different capillary designs a reliable fluid dynamic model should be established to propose possible designs for microflow-capillaries. Later on, the model should become a valuable tool for the further optimization of minimized capillary designs.

6. Improvement of the electrochemical control and optimization of the experimental parameters during the adaptation. This includes a further minimization of electrostatic interferences as well as an installation of an appropriate shielding concept to minimize noise for electrochemical measurements.

7. Installation of an observation unit to position and adjust the microflow-capillary on the sample.

Summary and Outlook

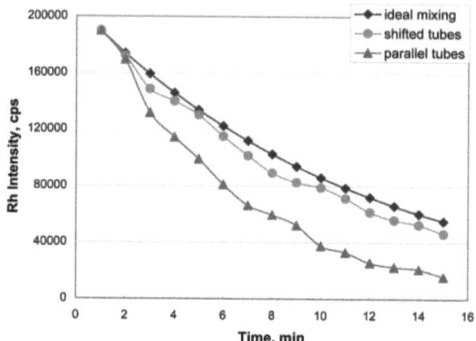

Fig. 6.1. Tracer-experiments, using Rh 10 µg L-1 as a tracer to evaluate the mixing capabilities in the microflow-capillary.

8. Concepts for a multi-microflow-capillary tool for simultaneous multi-position analysis on samples.

9. Concepts for scanning capabilities of the microflow-capillary on the surface

10. Application of the technique in corrosion analysis of new prospective materials are planned, *e.g.* the investigation of Mg-biodegradable alloys proposed for the temporary implants, pins or stents for bone fracture stabilization. Information on element- and time-dependent dissolution behaviour in different corrosive media is important to assess biocompatibility. The information about preferential metal ions' release is crucial for toxicity evaluation of these systems. Fig. 6.2 demonstrates the first results of the element-specific dissolution behaviour of Mg-Y alloy in comparison to pure magnesium. Based on these data a manuscript is currently in preparation (N.-C. Quach, N. Homazava, A. Ulrich, A. Bakken, P. Ugowitzer, P. Schmutz, Influence of ionic species present in body fluids on bio-corrosive mechanisms of Mg-Y-REE-alloys, planned for *Electrochimica Acta* 2009, in preparation.)

Summary and Outlook

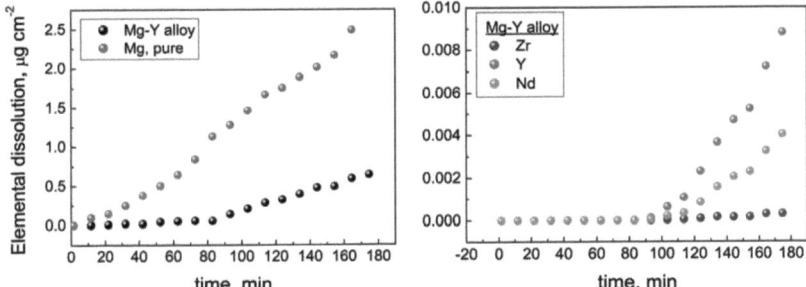

Fig 6.2. Element-specific dissolution rates of pure Mg in comparison to Mg-Y biodegradable alloy in 0.154 M NaCl solution.

11. Application of the microflow-capillary for non-conductive samples such as polymer samples or glasses.

7. Abbreviation list

AA – Al alloy

AAS – Atomic absorption spectrometry

AES – Auger electron spectroscopy

AFM – Atomic force microscopy

CE – Counter electrode

DL – Detection limit

EDX – Energy dispersive X-ray analysis

FI – Flow injection

FIAS – Flow injection analysis system

FI-ICP-MS - Flow injection inductively coupled plasma mass spectrometry

GDP – Gross domestic product

IC – Ion chromatography

ICP-MS - Inductively coupled plasma mass spectrometry

ICP-OES - Inductively coupled plasma optical emission spectrometry

ICP-QMS – Quadrupole inductively coupled plasma mass spectrometry

ICP-SFMS – Sector field inductively coupled plasma mass spectrometry

IMP – Intermetallic particle

LA-ICP-MS – Laser ablation inductively coupled plasma mass spectrometry

LF – Linear function

MDL –Method detection limit

MMN – Micromist nebulizer

OCP – Open circuit potential

PP – Polypropylene

Abbreviation list

PSIM - Phase shifting interferometric microscopy

PVC – Polyvinyl chloride

RE – Reference electrode

RSD – Relative standard deviation

SD – Standard deviation

SEM-EDX - Scanning electron microscopy coupled with energy dispersive X-ray analysis

SIMS - Secondary ion mass spectrometry

SKPFM - Scanning Kelvin probe force microscopy

TDS – Total dissolved salts

TEM-EDX – Transmission electron microscopy coupled with energy dispersive X-ray analysis

WE – Working electrode

XRD – X-ray diffraction

XPS - X-ray photoelectron spectroscopy

Zr-BMG – Zirconium bulk metallic glass

8. References.

[1] M. Pourbaix, Atlas of Electrochemical Equilibria, Brussels, 1974.
[2] H.H. Uhlig, The Cost of Corrosion in the United States, Chemical and Engineering News 27 (1949) 2764.
[3] U.S. Federal Highway Administration, Corrosion Costs and Preventative Strategies in the United States, Report FHWA-RD-01-156, 2002.
[4] Committee on Cost of Corrosion in Japan, Report on Cost of Corrosion in Japan, Japan Society of Corrosion Engineering and Japan Association of Corrosion Control, 2001.
[5] http://www.sulzerinnotec.com.
[6] M. Fontana, Corrosion Engineering, 3rd edition, McGraw Hill International Edition, New York, 1987.
[7] S.C. Thomas, V.I. Birss, Oxide film formation at a microcrystalline Al alloy in room temperature neutral borate solution, *Journal of the Electrochemical Society* 144 (1997) 558-566.
[8] A. Nylund, I. Olefjord, Surface analysis of oxidized aluminum. 1. Hydration of Al_2O_3 and decomposition of $Al(OH)_3$ in a vacuum as studied by ESCA, *Surface and Interface Analysis* 21 (1994) 283-289.
[9] I. Olefjord, A. Nylund, Surface analysis of oxidized aluminum. 2. Oxidation of aluminum in dry and humid atmosphere studied by ESCA, SEM, SAM and EDX, *Surface and Interface Analysis* 21 (1994) 290-297.
[10] S. Feliu Jr, M.J. Bartolome, Influence of alloying elements and etching treatment on the passivating films formed on aluminium alloys, *Surface and Interface Analysis* 39 (2007) 304-316.
[11] S. Scotto-Sheriff, E. Darque-Ceretti, G. Plassart, M. Aucouturier, Physico-chemical characterisation of native air-formed oxide films on Al-Mg alloys at low temperature. Influence of water, *Journal of Materials Science* 34 (1999) 5081-5088.
[12] S.K. Sharma, T. Strunskus, H. Ladebusch, F. Faupel, Surface oxidation of amorphous $Zr_{65}Cu_{17.5}Ni_{10}Al_{17.5}$ and $Zr_{46.75}Ti_{8.25}Cu_{7.5}Ni_{10}Be_{27.5}$, *Materials Science and Engineering: A* 304-306 (2001) 747-752.
[13] A. Dhawan, V. Zaporojtchenko, F. Faupel, S.K. Sharma, Study of air oxidation of amorphous $Zr_{65}Cu_{17.5}Ni_{10}Al_{7.5}$ by X-ray photoelectron spectroscopy (XPS), *Journal of Materials Science* 42 (2007) 9037-9044.
[14] Z. Szklarska-Smialowska, Pitting corrosion of aluminum, *Corrosion Science* 41 (1999) 1743-1767.
[15] N. Birbilis, R.G. Buchheit, Electrochemical characteristics of intermetallic phases in aluminum alloys: An experimental survey and discussion, *Journal of the Electrochemical Society* 152 (2005) B140-B151.
[16] N. Birbilis, R.G. Buchheit, Investigation and discussion of characteristics for intermetallic phases common to aluminum alloys as a function of solution pH, *Journal of the Electrochemical Society* 155 (2008) C117-C126.
[17] J.R. Scully, A. Gebert, J.H. Payer, Corrosion and related mechanical properties of bulk metallic glasses, *Journal of Materials Research* 22 (2007) 302-313.
[18] J. R. Davis, Corrosion: Understanding the Basics, 2nd edition, ASM International, 2000.

References

[19] H. Bohni, T. Suter, A. Schreyer, Micro- and nanotechniques to study localized corrosion, *Electrochimica Acta* 40 (1995) 1361-1368.

[20] T. Suter, H. Böhni, Microelectrodes for studies of localized corrosion processes, *Electrochimica Acta* 43 (1998) 2843-2849.

[21] T. Suter, H. Böhni, Microelectrodes for corrosion studies in microsystems, *Electrochimica Acta* 47 (2001) 191-199.

[22] T. Suter, Y. Müller, P. Schmutz, O. Von Trzebiatowski, Microelectrochemical studies of pit initiation on high purity and ultra high purity aluminum, *Advanced Engineering Materials* 7 (2005) 339-348.

[23] T. Suter, E.G. Webb, H. Böhni, R.C. Alkire, Pit Initiation on Stainless Steels in 1 M NaCl with and Without Mechanical Stress, *Journal of the Electrochemical Society* 148 (2001) B174-B185.

[24] T. Suter, R.C. Aikire, Microelectrochemical studies of pit initiation at single inclusions in Al 2024-T3, *Journal of the Electrochemical Society* 148 (2001) B36-B42.

[25] T. Suter, P. Schmutz, O.V. Trzebiatowski, Electrochemical characterization of submicrometer structures, *ECS Transactions* 3 (2007) 29-37.

[26] T. Hamelmann, M.M. Lohrengel, Electrochemical investigations of single microparticles, *Electrochimica Acta* 47 (2001) 117-120.

[27] M.M. Lohrengel, A. Moehring, M. Pilaski, Capillary-based droplet cells: Limits and new aspects, *Electrochimica Acta* 47 (2001) 137-141.

[28] V. Vignal, H. Krawiec, O. Heintz, R. Oltra, The use of local electrochemical probes and surface analysis methods to study the electrochemical behaviour and pitting corrosion of stainless steels, *Electrochimica Acta* 52 (2007) 4994-5001.

[29] J.O. Park, H. Böhni, Local pH measurements during pitting corrosion at MnS inclusions on stainless steel, *Electrochemical and Solid-State Letters* 3 (2000) 416-417.

[30] C.H. Paik, R.C. Alkire, Role of Sulfide Inclusions on Localized Corrosion of Ni200 in NaCl Solutions, *Journal of the Electrochemical Society* 148 (2001) B276-B281.

[31] R. Oltra, Local Electrochemical Methods in Corrosion Research, in Local Probe Techniques for Corrosion Research, Editors R. Oltra, V. Maurice, R. Akid and P. Marcus, CRS Press, 2007, 4-10.

[32] D.T. Larson, Surface analytic techniques in corrosion science, *Corrosion Science* 19 (1979) 657-673.

[33] N.S. McIntyre, D. Johnston, W.J. Chauvin, F.E. Doern, T.C. Chan, E. McAlpine, D. Lister, V.S. Shastri, Analysis of corrosion and oxidation on metals by spectroscopic means, *Fresenius' Zeitschrift für Analytische Chemie* 324 (1986) 625-634.

[34] M.J. Graham, 2003 W.R. Whitney Award Lecture: Application of surface techniques in understanding corrosion phenomena and oxide growth mechanisms, *Corrosion* 59 (2003) 475-488.

[35] http://www.eaglabs.com.

[36] P. Marcus, F. Mansfeld (Eds.), Analytical Methods in Corrosion Science and Engineering, CRC Taylor and Francis, 2005.

[37] A.V. Izmer, M.V. Zoriy, C. Pickhardt, W. Quadakkers, V. Shemet, L. Singheiser, J.S. Becker, LA-ICP-MS studies of cross section of NiCrAlY-based coatings on high-temperature alloys, *Journal of Analytical Atomic Spectrometry* 20 (2005) 918-923.

References

[38] A.G. Coedo, T. Dorado, I. Padilla, J.C. Farinas, Study of heterogeneities in steels and determination of soluble and total aluminium and titanium concentration by laser ablation inductively coupled plasma mass spectrometry, *Talanta* 71 (2007) 2108-2120.
[39] C. Latkoczy, T. Ghislain, Simultaneous LIBS and LA-ICP-MS analysis of industrial samples, *Journal of Analytical Atomic Spectrometry* 21 (2006) 1152-1160.
[40] C. Latkoczy, Y. Muller, P. Schmutz, D. Gunther, Quantitative element mapping of Mg alloys by laser ablation ICP-MS and EPMA, *Applied Surface Science* 252 (2005) 127-132.
[41] F. Andreatta, H. Terryn, J.H.W. De Wit, Corrosion behaviour of different tempers of AA7075 aluminium alloy, *Electrochimica Acta* 49 (2004) 2851-2862.
[42] V. Guillaumin, G. Mankowski, Localized corrosion of 6056 T6 aluminium alloy in chloride media, *Corrosion Science* 42 (2000) 105-125.
[43] K.A. Yasakau, M.L. Zheludkevich, S.V. Lamaka, M.G.S. Ferreira, Role of intermetallic phases in localized corrosion of AA5083, *Electrochimica Acta* 52 (2007) 7651-7659.
[44] G.S. Chen, M. Gao, R.P. Wei, Microconstituent-Induced Pitting Corrosion in Aluminum Alloy 2024-T3, *Corrosion* 52 (1996) 8-15.
[45] A. Gebert, K. Mummert, J. Eckert, L. Schultz, A. Inoue, Electrochemical investigations on the bulk glass forming $Zr_{55}Cu_{30}Al_{10}Ni_5$ alloy, *Materials and Corrosion - Werkstoffe und Korrosion* 48 (1997) 293-297.
[46] A. Gebert, K. Buchholz, A.M. El-Aziz, J. Eckert, Hot water corrosion behaviour of Zr-Cu-Al-Ni bulk metallic glass, *Materials Science and Engineering A* 316 (2001) 60-65.
[47] L. Liu, C.L. Qiu, H. Zou, K.C. Chan, The effect of the microalloying of Hf on the corrosion behavior of ZrCuNiAl bulk metallic glass, *Journal of Alloys and Compounds* 399 (2005) 144-148.
[48] D. Zander, B. Heisterkamp, I. Gallino, Corrosion resistance of Cu-Zr-Al-Y and Zr-Cu-Ni-Al-Nb bulk metallic glasses, *Journal of Alloys and Compounds* 434-435 (2007) 234-236.
[49] V.R. Raju, U. Kühn, U. Wolff, F. Schneider, J. Eckert, R. Reiche, A. Gebert, Corrosion behaviour of Zr-based bulk glass-forming alloys containing Nb or Ti, *Materials Letters* 57 (2002) 173-177.
[50] S. Hiromoto, A.P. Tsai, M. Sumita, T. Hanawa, Effects of surface finishing and dissolved oxygen on the polarization behavior of $Zr_{65}Al_{7.5}Ni_{10}Cu_{17.5}$ amorphous alloy in phosphate buffered solution, *Corrosion Science* 42 (2000) 2167-2185.
[51] S. Hiromoto, A.P. Tsai, M. Sumita, T. Hanawa, Effect of chloride ion on the anodic polarization behavior of the $Zr_{65}Al_{7.5}Ni_{10}Cu_{17.5}$ amorphous alloy in phosphate buffered solution, *Corrosion Science* 42 (2000) 1651-1660.
[52] C.L. Qiu, L. Liu, M. Sun, S.M. Zhang, The effect of Nb addition on mechanical properties, corrosion behavior, and metal-ion release of ZrAlCuNi bulk metallic glasses in artificial body fluid, *Journal of Biomedical Materials Research - Part A* 75 (2005) 950-956.
[53] C. Blanc, S. Gastaud, G. Mankowski, Mechanistic studies of the corrosion of 2024 aluminum alloy in nitrate solutions, *Journal of the Electrochemical Society* 150 (2003) B396-B404
[54] O. Seri, Effect of NaCl concentration on the corrosion behavior of aluminum containing iron, *Corrosion Science* 36 (1994) 1789-1803.
[55] A. Montaser (Ed.), Inductively Coupled Plasma Mass Spectrometry, Wiley-VCH, New York, 1998, 16-31.
[56] D. Beauchemin, Inductively coupled plasma mass spectrometry, *Analytical Chemistry* 80 (2008) 4455-4486.

[57] S.R. Taylor, B.D. Chambers, Identification and characterization of nonchromate corrosion inhibitor synergies using high-throughput methods, *Corrosion* 64 (2008) 255-270.
[58] B.D. Chambers, S.R. Taylor, The high throughput assessment of aluminium alloy corrosion using fluorometric methods. Part I - Development of a fluorometric method to quantify aluminium ion concentration, *Corrosion Science* 49 (2007) 1584-1596.
[59] T.H. Huang, C.C. Yen, C.T. Kao, Comparison of ion release from new and recycled orthodontic brackets, *American Journal of Orthodontics and Dentofacial Orthopedics* 120 (2001) 68-75.
[60] E. Bernardi, C. Chiavari, B. Lenza, C. Martini, L. Morselli, F. Ospitali, L. Robbiola, The atmospheric corrosion of quaternary bronzes: The leaching action of acid rain, *Corrosion Science* 51 (2009) 159-170.
[61] W.F. Heung, Y.P. Yang, P.C. Wong, K.A.R. Mitchell, T. Foster, XPS and corrosion studies on zinc phosphate coated 7075-T6 aluminium alloy, *Journal of Materials Science* 29 (1994) 1368-1373.
[62] S.R. Sousa, M.A. Barbosa, The effect of hydroxyapatite thickness on metal ion release from stainless steel substrates, *Journal of Materials Science: Materials in Medicine* 6 (1995) 818-823.
[63] B.K. Nash, R.G. Kelly, Application of ion chromatography to corrosion studies, *Journal of Chromatography* 602 (1992) 135-140.
[64] A. Kolics, A.S. Besing, P. Baradlai, R. Haasch, A. Wieckowski, Effect of pH on Thickness and Ion Content of the Oxide Film on Aluminum in NaCl Media, *Journal of the Electrochemical Society* 148 (2001) B251-B259
[65] T. Asnino, N. Ohtsu, K. Wagatsuma, Trace analysis of released metallic ions in static immersion test for characterization of metallic biomaterials, *Materials Transactions* 49 (2008) 1342-1345.
[66] P. Milleding, C. Haraldsson, S. Karlsson, Ion leaching from dental ceramics during static in vitro corrosion testing, *Journal of Biomedical Materials Research* 61 (2002) 541-550.
[67] K. Ogle, S. Weber, Anodic dissolution of 304 stainless steel using atomic emission spectroelectrochemistry, *Journal of the Electrochemical Society* 147 (2000) 1770-1780.
[68] D. Hamm, K. Ogle, C.O. Olsson, S. Weber, D. Landolt, Passivation of Fe-Cr alloys studied with ICP-AES and EQCM, *Corrosion Science* 44 (2002) 1443-1456.
[69] G. Herting, I. Odnevall Wallinder, C. Leygraf, Factors that influence the release of metals from stainless steels exposed to physiological media, *Corrosion Science* 48 (2006) 2120-2132.
[70] C.T. Liu, J.K. Wu, Influence of pH on the passivation behavior of 254SMO stainless steel in 3.5% NaCl solution, *Corrosion Science* 49 (2007) 2198-2209.
[71] E. Tufekci, J.C. Mitchell, J.W. Olesik, W.A. Brantley, E. Papazoglou, P. Monaghan, Inductively coupled plasma-mass spectroscopy measurements of elemental release from 2 high-palladium dental casting alloys into a corrosion testing medium, *Journal of Prosthetic Dentistry* 87 (2002) 80-85.
[72] M.A. Ameer, E. Khamis, M. Al-Motlaq, Electrochemical behaviour of recasting Ni-Cr and Co-Cr non-precious dental alloys, *Corrosion Science* 46 (2004) 2825-2836.
[73] L. Liu, C.L. Qiu, M. Sun, Q. Chen, K.C. Chan, G.K.H. Pang, Improvements in the plasticity and biocompatibility of Zr-Cu-Ni-Al bulk metallic glass by the microalloying of Nb, *Materials Science and Engineering: A* 449-451 (2007) 193-197.
[74] S. Hochstrasser, Y. Mueller, C. Latkoczy, S. Virtanen, P. Schmutz, Analytical characterization of the corrosion mechanisms of WC-Co by electrochemical methods and inductively coupled plasma mass spectroscopy, *Corrosion Science* 49 (2007) 2002-2020.

[75] S. Hochstrasser-Kurz, D. Reiss, T. Suter, C. Latkoczy, D. Günther, S. Virtanen, P.J. Uggowitzer, P. Schmutz, ICP-MS, SKPFM, XPS, and microcapillary investigation of the local corrosion mechanisms of WC-Co hardmetal, *Journal of the Electrochemical Society* 155 (2008) C415-C426.
[76] R.S. Houk, Inductively Coupled Argon Plasma as an Ion Source for Mass Spectrometric Determination of Trace Elements, *Analytical Chemistry* 52 (1980) 2283-2289.
[77] A.R. Date, A.L. Gray, Plasma source mass spectrometry using an inductively coupled plasma and a high resolution quadrupole mass filter, *The Analyst* 106 (1981) 1255-1267.
[78] S. M. Nelms (Ed.), Inductively Coupled Plasma Mass Spectrometry Handbook, Blackwell Publishing, Oxford, 2005.
[79] J.L. Todoli, J.M. Mermet, Elemental analysis of liquid microsamples through inductively coupled plasma spectrochemistry, *TrAC - Trends in Analytical Chemistry* 24 (2005) 107-116.
[80] J. Mora, S. Maestre, V. Hernandis, J.L. Todoli, Liquid-sample introduction in plasma spectrometry, *TrAC - Trends in Analytical Chemistry* 22 (2003) 123-132.
[81] http://www.geicp.com.
[82] J.L. Todoli, S. Maestre, J. Mora, A. Canals, V. Hernandis, Comparison of several spray chambers operating at very low liquid flow rates in inductively coupled plasma atomic emission spectrometry, *Fresenius' Journal of Analytical Chemistry* 368 (2000) 773-779.
[83] S.E. Maestre, J.L. Todoli, J.M. Mermet, Evaluation of several pneumatic micronebulizers with different designs for use in ICP-AES and ICP-MS. Future directions for further improvement, *Analytical and Bioanalytical Chemistry* 379 (2004) 888-899.
[84] B. Langlois, J.L. Dautheribes, J.M. Mermet, Comparison of a direct injection nebulizer and a micronebulizer associated with a spray chamber for the determination of iodine in the form of volatile CH_3I by inductively coupled plasma sector field mass spectrometry, *Journal of Analytical Atomic Spectrometry* 18 (2003) 76-79.
[85] M. Haldimann, A. Eastgate, B. Zimmerli, Improved measurement of iodine in food samples using inductively coupled plasma isotope dilution mass spectrometry, *Analyst* 125 (2000) 1977-1982.
[86] J.L. Todoli, J.M. Mermet, Sample introduction systems for the analysis of liquid microsamples by ICP-AES and ICP-MS, *Spectrochimica Acta Part B: Atomic Spectroscopy* 61 (2006) 239-283.
[87] J. Ruzicka, E.H. Hansen, Flow injection analyses. Part I. A new concept of fast continuous flow analysis, *Analytica Chimica Acta* 78 (1975) 145-157.
[88] G.D. Christian, J. Ruzicka, Flow injection analysis: a novel tool for plasma spectroscopy, *Spectrochimica Acta Part B: Atomic Spectroscopy* 42 (1987) 157-167.
[89] C.W. McLeod, Flow injection techniques in inductively coupled plasma spectrometry: Plenary lecture, *Journal of Analytical Atomic Spectrometry* 2 (1987) 549-552.
[90] J.R. Dean, L. Ebdon, H.M. Crews, R.C. Massey, Characteristics of flow injection inductively coupled plasma mass spectrometry for trace metal analysis, *Journal of Analytical Atomic Spectrometry* 3 (1988) 349-354.
[91] R.H. Scott, V.A. Fassel, R.N. Kniseley, D.E. Nixon, Inductively coupled plasma-optical emission analytical spectrometry: A compact facility for trace analysis of solutions, *Analytical Chemistry* 46 (1974) 75-80.
[92] R. Thomas, Beginner's Guide to ICP-MS, *Spectroscopy* 16 (2001) 26-30.
[93] P. H. Dawson, N. R. Whetten, Mass spectroscopy using rf quadrupole fields, *Advances in Electronics and Electron Physics* 27 (1969) 59-185.

[94] W. Paul and M. Raether, Das Electrische Massenfilter, *Zeitschrift für Physik* 140 (1955) 262-271.
[95] N. Bradshaw, E.F.H. Hall, N.E. Sanderson, Inductively coupled plasma as an ion source for high-resolution mass spectrometry, *Journal of Analytical Atomic Spectrometry* 4 (1989) 801-803.
[96] N. Jakubowski, L. Moens, F. Vanhaecke, Sector field mass spectrometers in ICP-MS, *Spectrochimica acta, Part B: Atomic spectroscopy* 53 (1998) 1739-1763.
[97] R.E. Sturgeon, J.W.H. Lam, A. Saint, Analytical characteristics of a commercial ICP orthogonal acceleration time-of-flight mass spectrometer (ICP-TOFMS), *Journal of Analytical Atomic Spectrometry* 15 (2000) 607-616.
[98] D.P. Myers, G. Li, P.P. Mahoney, G.M. Hieftje, An inductively coupled plasma-time-of-flight mass spectrometer for elemental analysis. Part III: Analytical performance, *Journal of the American Society for Mass Spectrometry* 6 (1995).
[99] G.M. Hieftje, Emergence and impact of alternative sources and mass analyzers in plasma source mass spectrometry, *Journal of Analytical Atomic Spectrometry* 23 (2008) 661-672.
[100] R. Thomas, A beginner's guide to ICP-MS: Part X - Detectors, *Spectroscopy* 17 (2002) 34-39.
[101] E.H. Evans, J.J. Giglio, Interferences in inductively coupled plasma mass spectrometry. A review, *Journal of Analytical Atomic Spectrometry* 8 (1993) 1-18.
[102] T.W. May, R.H. Wiedmeyer, A Table of Polyatomic Interferences in ICP-MS, *Atomic Spectroscopy* 19 (1998) 150-155.
[103] I. Rodushkin, T. Ruth, D. Klockare, Non-spectral interferences caused by a saline water matrix in quadrupole and high resolution inductively coupled plasma mass spectrometry, *Journal of Analytical Atomic Spectrometry* 13 (1998) 159-166.
[104] H. Falk, R. Geerling, B. Hattendorf, K. Krengel-Rothensee, K.P. Schmidt, Capabilities and limits of ICP-MS for direct determination of element traces in saline solutions, *Fresenius' Journal of Analytical Chemistry* 359 (1997) 352-356.
[105] N.M. Reed, R.O. Cairns, R.C. Hutton, Y. Takaku, Characterization of polyatomic ion interferences in inductively coupled plasma mass spectrometry using a high resolution mass spectrometer, *Journal of Analytical Atomic Spectrometry* 9 (1994) 881-896.
[106] F. Laborda, M.P. Gorriz, E. Bolea, J.R. Castillo, Mathematical correction for polyatomic interferences in the speciation of chromium by liquid chromatography-inductively coupled plasma quadrupole mass spectrometry, *Spectrochimica Acta - Part B Atomic Spectroscopy* 61 (2006) 433-437.
[107] S. Catarino, A.S. Curvelo-Garcia, R.B.d. Sousa, Measurements of contaminant elements of wines by inductively coupled plasma-mass spectrometry: A comparison of two calibration approaches, *Talanta* 70 (2006) 1073-1080.
[108] H. Vanhoe, J. Goossens, L. Moens, R. Dams, Spectral interferences encountered in the analysis of biological materials by inductively coupled plasma mass spectrometry, *Journal of Analytical Atomic Spectrometry* 9 (1994) 177-185.
[109] N. Violante, F. Petrucci, P. Delle Femmine, S. Caroli, Study of Possible Polyatomic Interference in the Determination of Cr in Some Environmental Matrices by Inductively Coupled Plasma Mass Spectrometry, *Microchemical Journal* 59 (1998) 269-277.
[110] M. Segura, Y. Madrid, C. Camara, Elimination of calcium and argon interferences in iron determination by ICP-MS using desferrioxamine chelating agent immobilized in sol-gel and cold plasma conditions, *Journal of Analytical Atomic Spectrometry* 18 (2003) 1103-1108.

[111] K.H. Lee, M. Oshima, S. Motomizu, Inductively coupled plasma mass spectrometric determination of heavy metals in sea-water samples after pre-treatment with a chelating resin disk by an on-line flow injection method, *Analyst* 127 (2002) 769-774.
[112] H.H. Chen, D. Beauchemin, Determination of trace metals in saline water using flow injection on-line precipitation coupled with inductively coupled plasma mass spectrometry, *Journal of Analytical Atomic Spectrometry* 16 (2001) 1356-1363.
[113] Y. Gao, K. Oshita, K.H. Lee, M. Oshima, S. Motomizu, Development of column-pretreatment chelating resins for matrix elimination/multi-element determination by inductively coupled plasma-mass spectrometry, *Analyst* 127 (2002) 1713-1719.
[114] C. Vandecasteele, M. Nagels, H. Vanhoe, R. Dams, Suppression of analyte signal in inductively-coupled plasma/mass spectrometry and the use of an internal standard, *Analytica Chimica Acta* 211 (1988) 91-98.
[115] D. G. Altenpohl, Aluminum: Technology, Applications, and Environment, TMS, 1998.
[116] W.H. Wang, C. Dong, C.H. Shek, Bulk metallic glasses, *Materials Science and Engineering: R* 44 (2004) 45-89.
[117] J.F. Löffler, Bulk metallic glasses, *Intermetallics* 11 (2003) 529-540.
[118] M. Telford, The case for bulk metallic glass, *Materials Today* 7 (2004) 36-43.
[119] J.A. Horton, D.E. Parsell, Biomedical potential of a zirconium-based bulk metallic glass, *Materials Research Society Symposium - Proceedings* 754 (2003) 179-184.
[120] N. Homazava, A. Ulrich, M. Trottmann, U. Krahenbuhl, Micro-capillary system coupled to ICP-MS as a novel technique for investigation of micro-corrosion processes, *Journal of Analytical Atomic Spectrometry* 22 (2007) 1122-1130.
[121] F. Eckermann, P.J. Uggowitzer, P. Schmutz, Influence of Composition and Roughness on Localized Corrosion of Al-Mg-Si alloys Characterized by Microelectrochemistry, *Materials Science Forum* 519-521 (2006) 635-640.
[122] B.S. Tanem, G. Svenningsen, J. Mardalen, Relations between sample preparation and SKPFM Volta potential maps on an EN AW-6005 aluminium alloy, *Corrosion Science* 47 (2005) 1506-1519.
[123] M. Gysler, Charakterisierung der Korrosionsbeständigkeit von Aluminiumlegierungen, Diploma thesis, Zürcher Hochschule Winterthur, 2005.
[124] R. Figi, C. Schreiner, D. Bleiner, Systematic investigations of plastic vials concerning their suitability for ultratrace anion analysis in high-purity industrial applications, *Microchimica Acta* 150 (2005) 199-209.
[125] A. Afseth, J.H. Nordlien, G.M. Scamans, K. Nisancioglu, Influence of heat treatment and surface conditioning on filiform corrosion of aluminium alloys AA3005 and AA5754, *Corrosion Science* 43 (2001) 2359-2377.
[126] M.A. Alodan, W.H. Smyrl, Detection of localized corrosion of aluminum alloys using fluorescence microscopy, *Journal of the Electrochemical Society* 145 (1998) 1571-1577.
[127] C.J. Boxley, H.S. White, Relationship between Al_2O_3 film dissolution rate and the pitting potential of aluminum in NaCl solution, *Journal of the Electrochemical Society* 151 (2004) B265-B270.
[128] P. Schmutz, G.S. Frankel, Characterization of AA2024-T3 by scanning Kelvin probe force microscopy, *Journal of the Electrochemical Society* 145 (1998) 2285-2295.
[129] P. Schmutz, G.S. Frankel, Corrosion study of AA2024-T3 by scanning Kelvin probe force microscopy and in situ atomic force microscopy scratching, *Journal of the Electrochemical Society* 145 (1998) 2295-2306.

[130] N. Homazava, A. Ulrich, U. Krähenbühl, Spatially and time-resolved element-specific in situ corrosion investigations with an online hyphenated microcapillary flow injection inductively coupled plasma mass spectrometry set-up., *Spectrochimica Acta Part B* 63 (2008) 777-783.
[131] P.M. Sarradin, N. Le Bris, C. Le Gall, P. Rodier, Fe analysis by the ferrozine method: Adaptation to FIA towards in situ analysis in hydrothermal environment, *Talanta* 66 (2005) 1131-1138.
[132] M. Silva, K. Kyser, D. Beauchemin, Enhanced flow injection leaching of rocks by focused microwave heating with in-line monitoring of released elements by inductively coupled plasma mass spectrometry, *Analytica Chimica Acta* 584 (2007) 447-454.
[133] Y.C. Sun, Y.W. Lu, Y.T. Chung, Online in-tube solid phase extraction coupled to ICP-MS for in vivo determination of the transfer kinetics of trace elements in the brain extracellular fluid of anesthetized rats, *Journal of Analytical Atomic Spectrometry* 22 (2007) 77-83.
[134] W.C. Tseng, Y.C. Sun, M.H. Yang, T.P. Chen, T.H. Lin, Y.L. Huang, On-line microdialysis sampling coupled with flow injection electrothermal atomic absorption spectrometry for in vivo monitoring of extracellular manganese in brains of living rats, *Journal of Analytical Atomic Spectrometry* 18 (2003) 38-43.
[135] C.J. Lin, M.H. Shao, Y.H. Lin, R.S. Huang, Y. Li, R.G. Du, Scanning electrochemical probes studies of localized corrosion and Ce inhibition for Al 2024 alloy in chloride solution, *Proceedings - Electrochemical Society* 23 (2003) 36-41.
[136] Y. Liu, X. Zhou, G.E. Thompson, T. Hashimoto, G.M. Scamans, A. Afseth, Precipitation in an AA6111 aluminium alloy and cosmetic corrosion, *Acta Materialia* 55 (2007) 353-360.
[137] A. Shi, B.A. Shaw, E. Sikora, The role of grain boundary regions in the localized corrosion of a copper-free 6111-like aluminum alloy, *Corrosion* 61 (2005) 534-547.
[138] N. Homazava, A. Shkabko, D. Logvinovich, U. Krähenbühl, A. Ulrich, Element-specific in situ corrosion behavior of Zr-Cu-Ni-Al-Nb bulk metallic glass in acidic media studied using a novel microcapillary flow injection inductively coupled plasma mass spectrometry technique, *Intermetallics* 16 (2008) 1066-1072.
[139] A. Inoue, Bulk Amorphous Alloys: Practical Characteristics and Applications, Trans Tech Publications, 1999.
[140] C.C. Hays, J. Schroers, U. Geyer, S. Bossuyt, N. Stein, W.L. Johnson, Glass forming ability in the Zr-Nb-Ni-Cu-Al bulk metallic glasses, *Materials Science Forum* 343-346 (2000) 103-108.
[141] A. Grimberg, H. Baur, P. Bochsler, F. Bühler, D.S. Burnett, C.C. Hays, V.S. Heber, A.J.G. Jurewicz, R. Wieler, Solar wind neon from genesis: Implications for the lunar noble gas record, *Science* 314 (2006) 1133-1135.
[142] A. Grimberg, H. Baur, F. Bühler, P. Bochsler, R. Wieler, Solar wind helium, neon, and argon isotopic and elemental composition: Data from the metallic glass flown on NASA's Genesis mission, *Geochimica et Cosmochimica Acta* 72 (2008) 626-645.
[143] C.L. Qiu, Q. Chen, L. Liu, K.C. Chan, J.X. Zhou, P.P. Chen, S.M. Zhang, A novel Ni-free Zr-based bulk metallic glass with enhanced plasticity and good biocompatibility, *Scripta Materialia* 55 (2006) 605-608.
[144] S. Buzzi, K. Jin, P.J. Uggowitzer, S. Tosatti, I. Gerber, J.F. Löffler, Cytotoxicity of Zr-based bulk metallic glasses, *Intermetallics* 14 (2006) 729-734.
[145] D. Zander, U. Köster, Corrosion of amorphous and nanocrystalline Zr-based alloys, *Materials Science and Engineering: A.* 375-377 (2004) 53-59.

[146] A. Dhawan, K. Sachdev, S. Roychowdhury, P.K. De, S.K. Sharma, Potentiodynamic polarization studies on amorphous $Zr_{46.75}Ti_{8.25}Cu_{7.5}Ni_{10}Be_{27.5}$, $Zr_{65}Cu_{17.5}Ni_{10}Al_{7.5}$, $Zr_{67}Ni_{33}$ and $Ti_{60}Ni_{40}$ in aqueous HNO3 solutions, *Journal of Non-Crystalline Solids* 353 (2007) 2619-2623.

[147] S. Pang, T. Zhang, H. Kimura, K. Asami, A. Inoue, Corrosion behavior of Zr-(Nb-)Al-Ni-Cu glassy alloys, *Materials Transactions, JIM* 41 (2000) 1490-1494.

[148] S.J. Pang, H. Men, C.H. Shek, C. Ma, A. Inoue, T. Zhang, Formation, thermal stability and corrosion behavior of glassy $Ti_{45}Zr_5Cu_{45}Ni_5$ alloy, *Intermetallics* 15 (2007) 683-686.

[149] N. Homazava, T. Suter, P. Schmutz, S. Toggweiler, A. Grimberg, U. Krähenbühl, A. Ulrich, Online hyphenation of potentiostat to a microflow-capillary FI-ICP-MS for simultaneous in situ electrochemical, time and element resolved characterization of local corrosion processes - An application for Zr-bulk metallic glass, *Journal of Analytical Atomic Spectrometry* (2009) submitted.

[150] A. Gebert, K. Buchholz, A. Leonhard, K. Mummert, J. Eckert, L. Schultz, Investigations on the electrochemical behaviour of Zr-based bulk metallic glasses, *Materials Science and Engineering A* 267 (1999) 294-300.

[151] U.K. Mudali, S. Baunack, J. Eckert, L. Schultz, A. Gebert, Pitting corrosion of bulk glass-forming zirconium-based alloys, *Journal of Alloys and Compounds* 377 (2004) 290-297.

[152] P. Vanysek in Handbook of Chemistry and Physics (74th ed.), ed. D.R. Lide, CRC Press, Boca Raton, 1993-1994.

[153] C. Alquier, M.T. Vandenborre, M. Henry, Synthesis of niobium pentoxide gels, *Journal of Non-Crystalline Solids* 79 (1986) 383-395.

[154] A.S. Solovkin, Z.N. Tsvetkova, The chemistry of aqueous solutions of zirconium salts (does the zirconyl ion exist?), *Russian Chemical Reviews* 31 (1962) 655-669.

[155] P. Plagemann, Untersuchungen zur Lochkorrosion von Kupferrohren in Trinkwasserinstallationen, Dissertation, RWTH Aachen, 2001.

[156] R.G. Buchheit, R.P. Grant, P.F. Hlava, B. McKenzie, G.L. Zender, Local dissolution phenomena associated with S phase (Al2CuMg) particles in aluminum alloy 2024-T3, *Journal of the Electrochemical Society* 144 (1997) 2621-2628.

[157] B.A. Green, H.M. Meyer, R.S. Benson, Y. Yokoyama, P.K. Liaw, C.T. Liu, A study of the corrosion behaviour of $Zr_{50}Cu_{(40-x)}Al_{10}Pd_x$ bulk metallic glasses with scanning Auger microanalysis, *Corrosion Science* 50 (2008) 1825-1832.

[158] H.B. Lu, L.C. Zhang, A. Gebert, L. Schultz, Pitting corrosion of Cu-Zr metallic glasses in hydrochloric acid solutions, *Journal of Alloys and Compounds* 462 (2008) 60-67.

References

Acknowledgements

Here I would like to thank all the people who helped, inspired and supported me during the time of my PhD project.

First of all I want to thank Prof. Dr. Urs Krähenbühl at the University of Bern for undertaking the academic supervision of my PhD thesis. Also I am grateful to him for very fruitful, comprehensive and supportive discussions.

Dr. Andrea Ulrich from Empa, I like to thank for the interesting thesis topic and for initializing financial support from Swiss National Science Foundation SNF. Moreover, I thank her for really valuable input and motivating ideas during the whole time of the PhD project, for introducing me to the world of ICP-MS and ICP-OES and for taking great care about correcting and improving my papers.

Prof. Dr. Thomas Wandlowski for agreeing to be a co-examiner at my PhD defence.

I am very grateful to our small Plasmaspectrometry group for a really nice and inspiring working atmosphere. Especially, I would like to thank Adrian Wichser for being always there when the help was needed, for great and useful advices in the lab and, of course, for great excursions in Zürich.

I would also like to thank Dr. Patrik Schmutz, Fabian Eckermann, Dr. Thomas Suter and Dr. Ngoc Quach for the fruitful collaboration and discussions on interpretation of corrosion mechanisms. Dr. Ansgar Grimberg and NASA's Genesis curation team for providing very valuable Zr-bulk metallic glass samples.

Special thanks go to Matthias Trottmann and Sven Toggweiler for their help in SEM-EDX measurements, Andrey Shkabko for his help in XPS measurements and my dear husband Dr. Dmitry Logvinovich for his professional support in XRD analysis.

I also would like to thank all the present and former members of the Laboratory for Analytical Chemistry: Dr. Heinz Vonmont, Harald Hagendorfer, Renato Figi, Oliver Nagel, Dr. Marianne Senn, Dr. Norbert Heeb, Claudia Müller, Dr. Peter Schmid and all other colleagues for a very friendly and supportive atmosphere during three and a half years of my stay at Empa

Acknowledgements

My special and true thanks also go to the colleagues and friends from the Solid State Chemistry group and PSI: Laura Bocher, Dr. Rosa Robert, Dr. Myriam Aguirre, Andrey Shkabko, Ivan Marozau, Dr. Anke Weidenkaff, Peter Tomes, Romain Fardel for nice atmosphere during the lunch breaks, for great parties organized and for not leaving me behind when our labs have split.

The financial support of the project from Swiss National Science Foundation (Project No. 200021-109355) is greatly acknowledged.

Last but not least, I want to thank my parents, my brother Pavel and my dear husband Dima for their deep and true support. Спасибо вам всем большое за настоящую любовь и заботу. За веру в меня и искреннюю поддержку.

List of publications

1. **N. Homazava**, A. Ulrich, M. Trottmann, U. Krähenbühl: Micro-capillary system coupled to ICP-MS as a novel technique for investigation of micro-corrosion processes, *Journal of Analytical Atomic Spectrometry* 22 (2007) 1122–1130.

2. **N. Homazava**, A. Ulrich, U. Krähenbühl: Spatially and time-resolved element-specific in situ corrosion investigations with an online hyphenated microcapillary FI-ICP-MS set-up, *Spectrochimica Acta Part B: Atomic Spectroscopy* 63 (2008) 777-783.

3. **N. Homazava**, A. Shkabko, D. Logvinovich, U. Krähenbühl, A. Ulrich: Element-specific in situ corrosion behavior of Zr-Cu-Ni-Al-Nb bulk metallic glass in acidic media studied using a novel microcapillary flow injection inductively coupled plasma mass spectrometry technique, *Intermetalics* 16 (2008) 1066-1072.

4. **N. Homazava**, A. Ulrich, U. Krähenbühl: In-situ element-specific and time-resolved investigation of micro-corrosion processes, *Chimia*, 62 (2008) 530.

5. **N. Homazava**, T. Suter, P. Schmutz, S. Toggweiler, A. Grimberg, U. Krähenbühl, A. Ulrich: Online hyphenation of potentiostat to a microflow-capillary flow injection ICP-MS for simultaneous in situ electrochemical, time- and element resolved characterization of local corrosion processes - An application for Zr-bulk metallic glass, *Journal of Analytical Atomic Spectrometry* (2009) accepted.

6. M. H. Aguirre, S. Canulescu, R. Robert, **N. Homazava**, D. Logvinovich, L. Bocher, Th. Lippert, M. Döbeli, A. Weidenkaff: Structure, microstructure, and high-temperature transport properties of $La_{1-x}Ca_xMnO_{3-\sigma}$ thin films and polycrystalline bulk materials, *Journal of Applied Physics*, 103 (2008) 013703.

7. D. Logvinovich, J. Hejtmanek, K. Knížek, M. Maryško, **N. Homazava**, P. Tomeš, R. Aguiar, S.G. Ebbinghaus, A. Reller, A. Weidenkaff: On the magnetism, thermal and electrical transport of $SrMoO_2N$, *Journal of Applied Physics* 105 (2009) 023522.

Contribution to the conferences and awards

1. **N. Homazava**, A. Ulrich, U. Krähenbühl: In situ element- and time-resolved corrosion investigations with an online hyphenated FI-ICP-MS capillary set-up (**poster**), Empa PhD day 2006, 21 November, 2006: Dübendorf, *Switzerland*, Best Poster Award.

2. **N. Homazava**, A. Ulrich, U. Krähenbühl: Element-Specific Investigation of Micro-corrosion Processes in Al Alloys by ICP-MS (**oral presentation**), 2007 European Plasma Winter Conference, 18–23 February 2007: Taormina, *Italy*.

3. **N. Homazava**, A. Ulrich, U. Krähenbühl: A Micro-capillary System Coupled to an ICP-MS as a Novel Technique for Investigation of Micro-corrosion Processes (**poster**), 2007 European Plasma Winter Conference, 18–23 February 2007: Taormina, *Italy*, JAAS Best Poster Award.

4. A. Ulrich, **N. Homazava**, U. Krähenbühl: Elementspezifische microanalytische in-situ-Untersuchungen von Korrosionsprozessen bei Aluminiumlegierungen mittels ICP-MS - Element-Specific Microanalytical in-situ investigation of Corrosion Processes for Aluminium Alloys using ICP-MS (**oral presentation**), CANAS 2007, 18-21 March 2007: Konstanz, *Germany*.

5. **N. Homazava**, A. Ulrich, U. Krähenbühl: Entwicklung eines neuartigen Mikrokapillar-Fliesszellen-Sysems gekoppelt mit ICP-MS zur elementspezifischen und ortsaufgelösten Untersuchung von lokalen Korrosionsprozessen -Development of a novel micro-capillary system coupled to an ICP-MS for spatially and element resolved investigation of corrosion processes (**poster**), CANAS 2007, 18-21 March 2007: Konstanz, *Germany*.

6. **N. Homazava**, U. Krähenbühl, A. Ulrich: Novel microcapillary FI-ICP-MS technique for in situ time- and element-resolved corrosion investigations (**oral presentation**), Third Asian Pacific Winter Conference on Plasma Mass Spectrometry 2008, 16-21 November 2008: Tsukuba, *Japan*.

7. **N. Homazava**, U. Krähenbühl, A. Ulrich: Time- and element-dependent corrosion behaviour of novel biocompatible materials studied using a novel microcapillary FI-ICP-MS set-up (**poster**), Third Asian Pacific Winter Conference on Plasma Mass Spectrometry 2008, 16-21 November 2008: Tsukuba, *Japan*.

Awards

1. *Best Poster Award* at Empa PhD day 2006 for the poster N. Homazava, A. Ulrich, U. Krähenbühl, Element-Specific Investigation of Micro-corrosion Processes in Al Alloys by ICP-MS.

2. *JAAS Poster Award* at 2007 European Plasma Winter Conference for the poster N. Homazava, A. Ulrich, U. Krähenbühl, A Micro-capillary System Coupled to an ICP-MS as a Novel Technique for Investigation of Micro-corrosion Processes.

Die VDM Verlagsservicegesellschaft sucht für wissenschaftliche Verlage abgeschlossene und herausragende

Dissertationen, Habilitationen, Diplomarbeiten, Master Theses, Magisterarbeiten usw.

für die kostenlose Publikation als Fachbuch.

Sie verfügen über eine Arbeit, die hohen inhaltlichen und formalen Ansprüchen genügt, und haben Interesse an einer honorarvergüteten Publikation?

Dann senden Sie bitte erste Informationen über sich und Ihre Arbeit per Email an *info@vdm-vsg.de*.

Sie erhalten kurzfristig unser Feedback!

VDM Verlagsservicegesellschaft mbH
Dudweiler Landstr. 99　　　　　　　Telefon　+49 681 3720 174
D - 66123 Saarbrücken　　　　　　　Fax　　　+49 681 3720 1749
www.vdm-vsg.de

Die VDM Verlagsservicegesellschaft mbH vertritt

Printed by Books on Demand GmbH, Norderstedt / Germany